How to Fail at Change Management

How to Fail at Change Management

A Manager's Guide to the Pitfalls of Managing Change

James Marion
John Lewis

BEP BUSINESS EXPERT PRESS

How to Fail at Change Management: A Manager's Guide to the Pitfalls of Managing Change
Copyright © Business Expert Press, LLC, 2020.

First published in 2020 by
Business Expert Press, LLC
222 East 46th Street, New York, NY 10017
www.businessexpertpress.com

ISBN-13: 978-1-95152-742-6 (paperback)
ISBN-13: 978-1-95152-743-3 (e-book)

Business Expert Press Portfolio and Project Management Collection

Collection ISSN: 2156-8189 (print)
Collection ISSN: 2156-8200 (electronic)

Cover image licensed by Ingram Image, StockPhotoSecrets.com

Cover and interior design by S4Carlisle Publishing Services Private Ltd., Chennai, India

First edition: 2020

10 9 8 7 6 5 4 3 2 1

Printed in the United States of America.

Abstract

Change management efforts often fail. Business case studies are littered with examples of failed change management efforts. Why this is so is a mystery, given the many change management models in existence, the highly paid executives equipped with degrees from top-tier schools, and that millions of dollars spent in pursuit of change. Successful change management need not be a mystery, but perhaps change management success is best learned from failed attempts at change that seemed reasonable at the time according to theory—but proved to be bad ideas in retrospect. This book presents notable examples of attempts by experienced managers to implement bad ideas that lead to failed change so that change managers are better equipped to avoid common pitfalls in managing change.

Keywords

change; change management; change management model; diagnosis

Contents

PART I

Change Models

Introduction to Part I

Change management initiatives do not fail because of the lack of change management models and frameworks. Many change management models exist that are widely promoted within both the field of change management consulting and academia. Further, an examination of most models does not appear to vary significantly from that which could be expected to arise from common sense. Prior to seeking to understand why change management fails, it is useful to understand typical change management frameworks that are in existence today.

CHAPTER 1

A Survey of Change and Change Models

Change Management and Common Sense: Things Change Managers Would Likely Do without Models

Physics informs us that "an object at rest tends to remain at rest; whereas an object in motion tends to remain in motion." Although the domain of organizational change management has little to do with physics, this principle does appear to readily apply. There is familiarity and comfort with adopting a routine and doing the same things in the same way over a long period of time. Changes made to the way things have always been done is uncomfortable for most employees. Discomfort leads to concern as well as uncertainty. Uncertainty about the future will always exist even when the news announcing change is apparently positive. Uncertainty then tends to fester over time and multiply as employees voice their concerns to one another in the hallways of the company and by the watercooler. Uncertainty reaches the point where it leads to fear—fear of the future and the unexpected. Fearful employees then seek to return to the comfort that they once knew, and in doing so, tend to resist the changes suggested by senior management. Change therefore tends to trigger a cycle of "routine, comfort, uncertainty, fear, and resistance." Managers attempting to change the organization to a new operation with improved performance and improved alignment with strategy are often at a loss at deciding how to succeed at creating such change. Change will always involve breaking with routine and introducing some level of uncertainty. Change managers will therefore encounter uncertainty, fear, and resistance regardless of the nature of the proposed change. They must expect it, prepare for it, and address it in change management initiatives.

Where to Start?

A start at creating change in the face of resistance might involve thinking about how to intervene in the negative spiral associated with the disruption of employees' comfortable routine. Common sense would suggest that as a fundamental first step, managers should attempt to clearly communicate the rationale behind the change that may be perceived by employees to be a disruption of a previous routine. Change management understand that there is a link between the discomfort of parting with the routine of today and the uncertainty associated with the new ways of doing things. It is paramount for managers to consider how to reduce uncertainty by painting a picture of what the future will look like, and how and why this is preferred over the routine of the past. Common sense would further dictate that managers would involve employees in some way in designing the change as well as in the implementation. Asking employees to go along with plans developed by someone else is far more difficult than assigning employees to contribute to the design and development of a plan that they would now consider to "own" even in some small way. To make an analogy, an airline pilot flying through a thunderstorm would be likely feel a greater sense of security than the typical passenger in the rear of the plane who is being jostled by the uncertainty of constant turbulence. The difference between the pilot and the passenger with respect to uncertainty and fear is the sense of control over one's own destiny. Stakeholders in change management initiatives who feel that they control their own destiny feel more like pilots than mere passengers.

In the same way that successful airline flights eventually find a way through the turbulence and land, change initiatives get carried out despite the headwinds and turbulence. Such changes are incorporated within the organization and feature revamped processes (Figure 1.1). It is at this point in the change process where the reality may not quite match the beautiful picture painted by managers. There will likely be growing pains that feature the desire to return to how things were done in the past. Once again, managers communicate on an ongoing basis the rationale behind the change, the promise that things will settle once again into routine, and that when they do, the future will be brighter than the past.

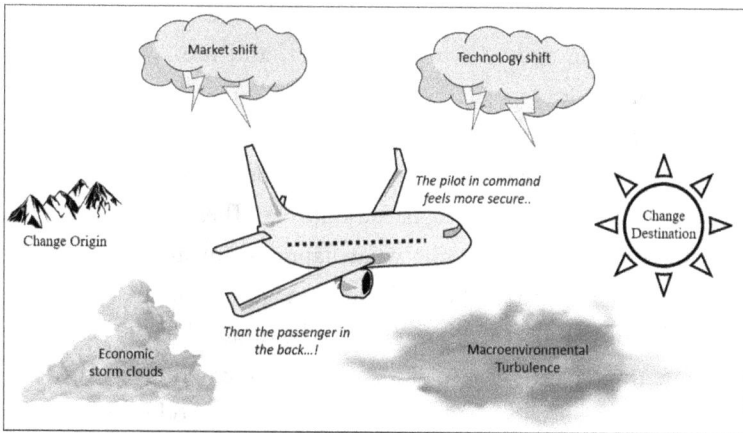

Figure 1.1 Change from the perspective of a pilot and passenger

How then does common sense inform executives and senior managers in the design and implementation of change initiatives? To summarize, it is all about effectively communicating the rationale behind the change, providing a clear description of an image of a better future, reducing uncertainty and fear by instilling employee ownership in the design and implementation of change, and finally continually reinforcing the change to ensure that employee buy-in continues. Common sense suggests that when many people will be affected by change, they should be informed and their input should be solicited. Understanding the relationship between change, uncertainty and resistance, fear, and day-to-day human behavior therefore leads to common-sense measures that work to reduce that almost automatic "push-back" from employees that is motivated by fear.

Change Management Models: What Are They and Why Use Them?

Though common sense provides guidance to managers who have it, formal academic models exist that seek to provide guidance and direction to managers who are more comfortable with following a prescribed series of steps to alter the current course of their organizations. Further, many managers do not have the time to think through a custom methodology for implementing change. Change managers need all the help and advice they can get, and they therefore reach out to thought leaders in the field for guidance. Academic models are attempts to not only explain what has happened when successful change was carried out, but what should happen as well. Some change management models tend to be descriptive. These models do little more than attempt to describe what happens during change. Other models are prescriptive. They inform managers what, in the view of the creator of the model, what "should" be done when initiating and implementing change. Often these models are based on hard experience from both success and failed change over a period of many years. Change management frameworks are also based on collected data from change managers to inform the researcher on what was done, how it was done along with results that inform what should be done as a matter of good practice. It pays to remember that these ideas are models of reality rather than reality itself. Change management models can work, but this is no guarantee that they always do work. The same could be said for most business practices. It depends on the context, how the practice is implemented, who implements it, and how well it is managed.

The Lewin Model: Unfreeze, Change, Refreeze

Lewin is a seminal author in the field of change management. Lewin informs us that change involves three steps—one of which—rather redundantly—is "change." The first step in the three-step process uses a term "unfreeze." To unfreeze an organization is to prepare it for change by breaking apart the legacy patterns of doing things. This is in effect taking "an object at rest" and giving it a push so that it is moving again. This is easier said than done given the natural uncertainty associated with change and the resulting resistance. However, common sense informs managers that a change effort cannot be completed unless it is first started, and unfreezing is starting the process. The real question is "how"? Unfreezing implies stopping something and taking a different action, for example, taking ice cubes out of the refrigerator and letting them melt.

For naturally talented leaders, the way to start is to put stakeholders at ease by sharing a vision for the future and including them in the change plan. In fact, such activity, reminiscent of unfreezing or melting ice cubes, is often referred to as "warming up." Ideally, unfreezing should result in receptive stakeholders who understand the intended change and the underlying rationale.

The next step in Lewin's framework is "change," but this is a single word that speaks volumes. The "change" phase focuses on implementing new processes, new practices, and new systems. There are many ways to do this, including training, practice, role-playing, and scenario planning, to name but a few. In most cases, things get worse before they get better as stakeholders gradually work through the discomfort of doing something in a new way. Eventually, if the change is successful, performance improves. Lewin then informs the manager that the change must "refreeze" into the organization. This term is shorthand for "institutionalizing the new way of doing things" (Figure 1.2). Once the company is familiar with the new way of doing things to the point that it is no longer new, and the application of new processes and systems comes naturally, it could be said that refreeze and institutionalization of the change has occurred.

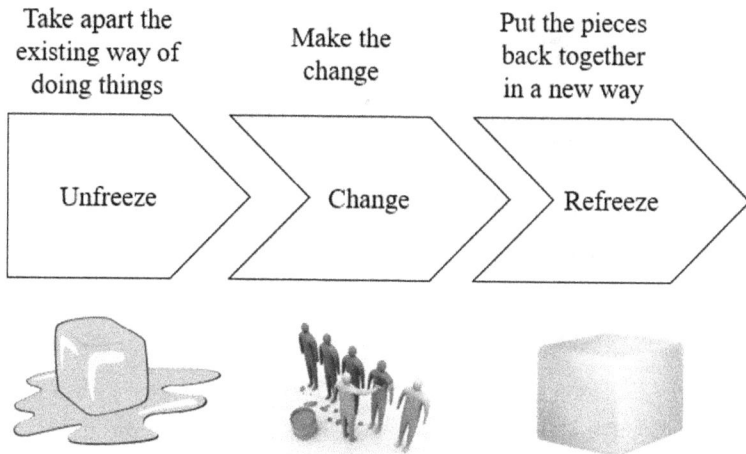

Figure 1.2 Lewin's model of managing change

Source: Lewin (1947).

Observations on Lewin

The Lewin framework expresses what is observed in common-sense thinking about managing change. Change must begin, it must be carried out, and the change must become a way of life. While the Lewin framework provides a structured path to follow when initiating and managing change, the phases are expressed in a compact form and require elaboration by any given manager. Presumably, effective managers could successfully employ Lewin, whereas others, following the same three phases, could easily fail and often do. It appears from inspection of the process that the Lewin framework could emerge from a common-sense consideration of what ought to happen within a change management scenario. Further, the three steps in the Lewin framework could be viewed as phases or categories of activities. Change managers could take this and develop a project around it. This could be done by identifying the desired deliverables from "unfreeze," "change," and "refreeze" followed by populating a schedule with activities and resources.

Kotter's Eight-Step Change Model

The Kotter's change model provides detail and structure far beyond the three-phase Lewin model. The eight steps are as follows:

1. Create urgency
2. Create a coalition
3. Develop a vision and strategy
4. Communicate the vision
5. Empower action
6. Get quick wins
7. Leverage wins to drive change
8. Embed in culture

An examination of the Kotter model suggests similarity with both a common-sense approach and the Lewin model, albeit with additional detail. Steps 1 to 4 appear to relate to preparing for change, "unfreezing," and reducing the uncertainty in the organization. Steps 5 to 7 involve carrying out the change by aiding the organization in getting things done while attempting to create a positive spiral of success. The implementation of change begins with things that can be accomplished quickly so that successes can raise the energy level and work to minimize the resistance to change. The thinking here is that resistance to change can be expected to decrease if positive results are observed by the stakeholders involved in change. Finally, new systems and processes are institutionalized by embedding the change in the culture, or in Lewin's terminology, "refreezing." "Embedding in culture" need not be a top-down effort from outside of the organized. Instead, it could be something that emerges from the practice of new processes, policies, and practices over time. In fact, this is known to occur in companies that exhibit an emergent strategy and culture rather than one dictated from the leadership level of the firm (Figure 1.3).

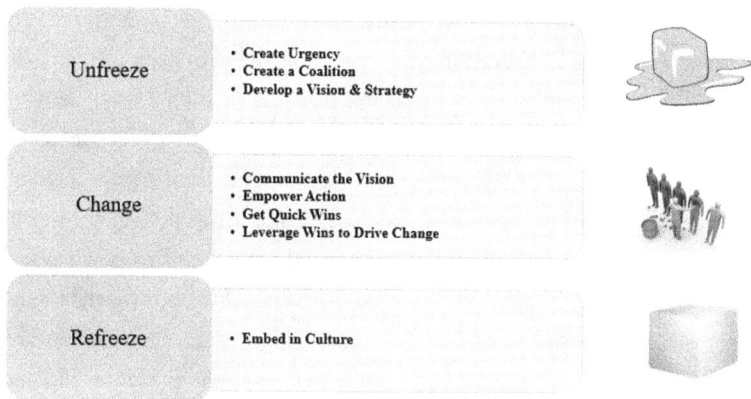

Unfreeze
- Create Urgency
- Create a Coalition
- Develop a Vision & Strategy

Change
- Communicate the Vision
- Empower Action
- Get Quick Wins
- Leverage Wins to Drive Change

Refreeze
- Embed in Culture

Figure 1.3 Kotter's eight-step model

Source: Kotter (2012).

Observations on Kotter

The Kotter model provides some interesting guidance to the manager. The first key point is that of urgency. It is observed that change leads to uncertainty and resistance that must be overcome by the change manager. Kotter makes the point that managers must not only answer the question of "Why change?" but also "Why change *now*?" The second key point that Kotter makes that extends the Lewin framework and the common-sense approach is to seek small victories or "quick wins" in order to provide evidence for the benefits of the proposed change as well as to build some positive momentum. The Kotter model is said to "extend" the Lewin model because although Kotter follow the general pattern of the fundamental stages of the Lewin framework, the Kotter model provides additional detail and guidance that in Lewin remains implicit.

PROSCI "ADKAR" and Three-Phase Model

PROSCI, an acronym for "professional science" is a consulting company dedicated to the art of change management. Two notable frameworks are promoted by PROSCI: the ADKAR and the three-phase change model. ADKAR is an acronym that stands for Awareness, Desire, Knowledge, Ability, and Reinforcement. The Awareness and Desire elements of ADKAR play a role in uncertainty reduction by reinforcing the need for change as well as describing the nature of the proposed change. The term "Desire" is aimed at engaging stakeholders in such a way that they support the change and want it to occur. Assuming that "Desire" is accomplished in the ADKAR framework, resistance to change will be likely to fade. On the other hand, desire and good intentions do not necessarily lead to results unless the appropriate know-how exist. This is where the "Knowledge" element comes into sharp focus. Once appropriate skills and behaviors are in place, the new knowledge combined with Awareness and Desire lead to Ability or the actual implementation of change. Finally, once the organization has changed, the new systems, processes, skills, and behaviors are Reinforced so that they become "frozen," "embedded" or institutionalized.

The ADKAR model reads much like a content model for change management as it lists all elements that should be included in a change management plan rather than describing the process steps to be carried out. PROSCI, however, also offers a three-phase process model that emphasizes the sequence of events in managed change. The PROSCI three-phase model is given as follows:

1. Preparing for change
   a. Define your change management strategy
   b. Prepare your change management teams
   c. Develop your sponsorship model

2. Managing change
   a. Develop change management plans
   b. Take action and implement plans
3. Reinforcing change
   a. Collect and analyze feedback
   b. Diagnose gaps and manage resistance
   c. Implement corrective actions and celebrate successes (Figure 1.4)

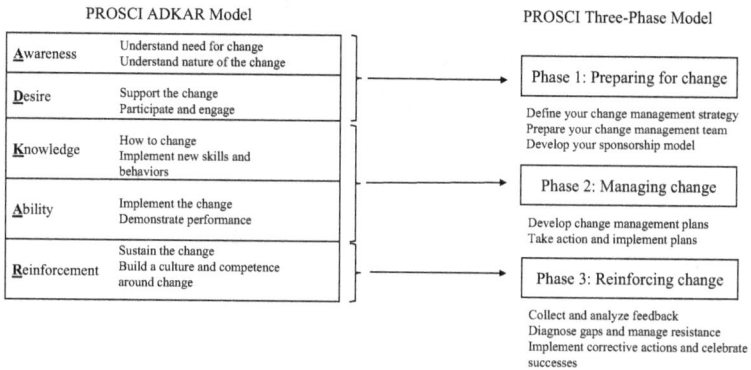

Figure 1.4 PROSCI and ADKAR

Source: Prosci (2019).

It is of interest to observe that the PROSCI three phases appear to mirror the Lewin model. Unlike Lewin, however, the three-phase model does not express the ideal of "refreezing" or "embedding" change, but rather appears to view change as something that requires ongoing management attention. Further, the initial phase emphasizes strategy, sponsorship, and teams. This suggests that initiating change must be supported with a clear plan of action, executive support in the form of sponsorship, and finally with teams of employees affected by the change.

Observations on PROSCI

PROSCI models have much in common with Lewin and Kotter. The three-phase model closely mirrors Lewin, with possible differences in how institutionalization of change is viewed. The ADKAR model is in apparent alignment with what common sense and other models would suggest. The initial elements of the model involve components tailored to the need for the reduction of uncertainty and resistance prior to implementation and institutionalizing of change. The ADKAR model stands out in its emphasis on the requirement for new knowledge and skills to support change. The desire to change without the requisite know-how increases the chances of failure. Further, the in-depth guidelines provided by PROSCI ring true as the result of significant experience and research.

McKinsey 7-S Model

Unlike other models, the 7-S presents an image of the key elements of the organization as well as how they are linked together. The 7-Ss are given as follows:

1. Shared values
2. Strategy
3. Structure
4. Systems
5. Style
6. Staff
7. Skills

Each of the Ss are connected directly or indirectly to other elements. This image suggests that a successful organization requires all elements to function well and to function well together. The 7-S framework is not so much a change management model per-se, but rather a guide for what to think about when embarking on change. The idea being expressed it that as each "S" connects to all other Ss, no "S" may be overlooked when embarking on change. The 7S model therefore appears to be a content rather than a process model for change. Unlike the phased approach of Lewin, the 7-S says little about where to start and finish, but rather what to include and what to think about when embarking upon a change management initiative (Figure 1.5).

Observations on 7-S

A concern of any model is that it is an attempt to represent reality with an idea or picture of the underlying reality. All models imperfectly

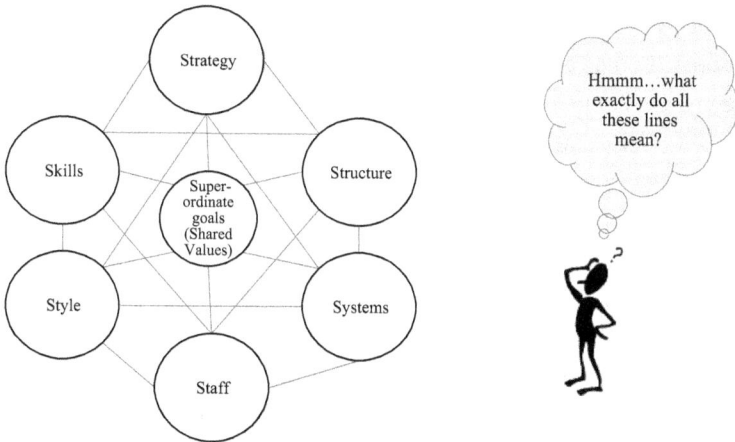

Figure 1.5 McKinsey 7-S model

Source: Jurevicius (2013).

characterize reality, but some models are better than others. Is the 7-S model "better"? The answer is "it depends." The right model used in change management could fail as a result of the wrong implementation. Also, thinking managers should carefully consider each proposed model in a critical manner. For example, McKinsey characterizes the firm in terms of "7-S," but then again, why does it have to be "7-Ss"? Why not 6 or 8? Or, 7-Ss and one A, N, or B? The 7-S content model of the firm may be considered a useful framework when applied in change management initiatives, but the result will depend on a well-thought-out execution. One example of this is the consideration of the linkages between each "S" in the model. What specifically are the links intended to convey? Are the linkages a general-purpose perspective on the components of all companies and how such components are linked? Do the links apply to your specific company? Should they? Finally, is each link intended to express one-way, two-way, or multi-way relationships? Managers would be well-advised to arrive at a clarity of understanding of the relationship of all elements of this model prior to attempting to implement it.

Senge and Systems Thinking

The "system thinking" of Senge appears to be related to the 7-S model in that Senge views the firm as an interconnected web. Unlike the 7-S model, Senge does not specify a list of connected functions, but rather emphasizes the connections between the functions. The firm is therefore viewed as a complex system with a significant number of feedback loops. Organizations tend to go off the track when leadership neglects or fails to understand the linkages and resulting feedback loops that exist. This is a cited reason for why new policies championed by leadership often fail. Further, Senge's view suggests that the documented organization chart does not accurately capture how individuals interact within an organization. A map of frequent connections between individuals and corresponding feedback loops would likely appear to be very different from the organization that is captured in the static organization chart. The organization should therefore be viewed as a complex system (Figure 1.6). It follows then that any changes to a complex system must be carefully considered and only undertaken when the system is fully understood. An analogy of the "organization" as system view could be provided in an automotive mechanic suggesting an action designed to improve engine performance. Engines have become more complex over time and as a result are controlled by microprocessors. Mechanics proposing change suggestions therefore require significant training, a holistic understanding of how the engine works, and certification. The Senge's view of the organization would appear to suggest that not everyone is qualified to suggest and implement organizational change. Perhaps it takes the organizational equivalent of a "certified mechanic."

Observations on Senge

While Senge does neither provide a process nor a content model for change, Senge does introduce a way of thinking essential to managers of change. Senge's view of organizations as systems reinforces the underlying cause for the "law of unintended consequences." That is, change initiatives embarked upon without an adequate level of understanding of the underly systems involved is bound to have unexpected results. Since change initiatives are known to fail with often spectacular unintended consequences, Senge's "system thinking" is a thoughtful approach for which change managers should seriously consider. The conceptual nature of the Senge systems' view of organizations is reminiscent of the theory

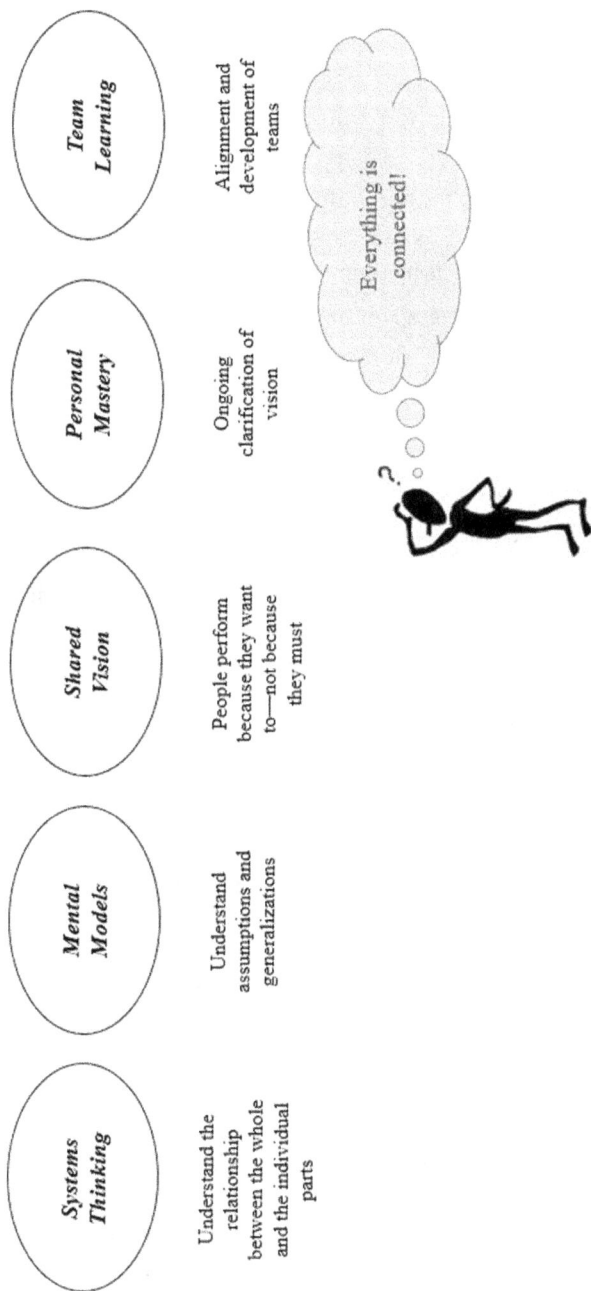

Figure 1.6 Senge and systems thinking

Source: Senge (1997).

of constraints philosophy introduced by Eli Goldratt in the seminal work "The Goal" first introduced in the late 1980s. Goldratt explains in this work that an operation can go no faster than the slowest element within the system. If a change manager wished, for example, to improve the output of a factory, the manager would identify the bottleneck or constraint, widen the bottleneck to improve overall throughput, and then finally identify and widen the next bottleneck using an iterative approach. A manager who took steps to increase output in an area of the factory in front of a bottleneck does little more than create unnecessary inventory. Like Senge, Goldratt proposes a means for developing insights regarding how the "pieces of the puzzle" fit together. Change managers who employ such conceptual models will have a better chance of identifying and solving the right problem.

Which Model Should Be Selected?

It is observed that change management models are many, yet successful change initiatives are few. From examination of well-known change models, it is observed that some describe a series of steps to be undertaken, whereas others suggest what change managers should consider when embarking upon change. Given that any change model may or may not succeed depending on the implementation of the change, managers could benefit from examining several different models such as have been presented in this text. A well-informed change manager might—rather than employ a single model—glean from the inspection of change models a few important guidelines to think about when initiating or managing change. Such guidelines might include the following:

1. Employ a systematic approach
2. Understand that a natural resistance to change exists in all organizations
3. Involve those who are affected by or have a stake in the change
4. Understand how the pieces fit together as well as how they interact
5. Make sure that you correctly understand the nature of the problem that your change initiative seeks to solve

CHAPTER 2

The Change Construct, Process, and Triggers

Is "Change Management" Too Big a Word?

An examination of the change management literature as well as the appeal to common sense illustrates a potential core problem with the concept of change management. Change management is a "construct." Although the word is defined as "the management of the planning and introduction of new methods, techniques, and processes in an organization," it is a single term that refers to many things and is therefore understood differently by different people. Also, when the term is used, it is not clear exactly what specific action should be taken. For example, if the executive were to tell an employee to "Start implementing change management tomorrow!" few would likely know exactly where to begin. Given that most change models, including a down-to-earth common-sense approach, involve a sequence of steps, change management is best envisioned as an emergent property arising from the completion of a number of steps. Perhaps "change management" is too big a word to use when embarking on change initiatives. Instead, greater understanding and less resistance may follow when the organization is led through a series of small steps. Once the last step has been executed, then it could be said that change management has emerged, at least for a time. Then, the next sequence of steps begins. To illustrate the underlying complexity of the change management construct, a word frequency analysis was undertaken by retrieving several articles, definitions, and commentaries on the subject of change management. The resulting word cloud with word size weighted by frequency of word appearance provides a graphical view of the many different viewpoints on the subject (Figure 2.1).

Figure 2.1 The many words of change management

Change as Problem-Solving

When caught up in the heat of the moment of a significant change initiative, it is not uncommon to wonder, "What problem is it that I am trying to solve?" Change is often triggered by a need to solve a problem in the organization. The problem may be generally spoken of in the hallways of the company, but when it comes to addressing it, the definition and analysis of the problem may become a bit "fuzzy." It is as this point that a manager could clarify the reason for the need to change by stating: "The problem I am attempting to solve is _____," or "The specific issue I am attempting to address is _____."

There is the old saying that it is "hard to be easy," or rather "it is difficult to be simple." Yet, the inability to express a problem in a succinct and clear way suggests that the problem is yet to be fully understood. The simple exercise of stating the problem is best done in writing. It could be written on a piece of paper, on a computer screen, or on a white board in front of a team. The key is that writing involves thinking. Notice how writing stops and then pen or chalk or keyboard is put away when an unclear point is reached. What happens next? A pause to more fully consider the intended point. The key to remember is that clarity is given in any change effort and succinctly stating the problem in writing helps achieve it.

The problem-solving paradigm may be useful when presenting the need for change to organizational stakeholders. Instead of promoting change, promote the specific problems that need solutions, and then propose solutions and request stakeholder input on such solutions. The solutions could be viewed as change initiatives, but if considered strictly as efforts taken to solve problems, buy-in from stakeholders may be more readily attained. It is one thing to hear about change, grow concerned, and then resist it, but quite another to be convinced the problems exists and that stakeholders are invited to join in the development of a solution.

When and Why to Change?

Although change management initiatives are frequently linked to problem-solving, this is not always the case. Change could be triggered by a major shift in the macroenvironment of the firm. For example, an important client could go out of business, there could be a major shift in interest rates, or perhaps two major competitors merge thereby creating market efficiencies that cause the market price levels to dramatically shift. The cause of the external trigger always varies, but it is a fact that the macro environment can be turbulent and companies must change accordingly or face failure as a business. The disruption caused by technology is also a trigger of change. Consider, for example, the rise of video streaming services and the resulting fall of cable television services and video rentals. Finally, change may be triggered internally, for example, the loss of a key employee or the recognition that the current organization is not producing optimal results or is not keeping up with changes in the marketplace. Rather internal or external, the answer to the question of "When and why?" when it comes to a change management is that change is often a response to a problem, issue, situation, or event. Change is therefore said to be "triggered." In this sense, change is a response to a stimulus. The problem with stimulus–response change to the organizational structure, to the product line, or to business systems is that they are usually triggered by a lack of competitiveness. When this is the case, management becomes aware of the need because sales are falling, expenses are increasing, and morale is low. This situation is analogous to making the decision to embark on a mountainous travel route upon discovering that the car is almost out of gas and the engine needs an oil change. Change requires funding and it requires energy; so as a result, change initiated during a time of decline and crisis is a high-risk endeavor that is not likely to succeed (Figure 2.2).

External

- Recession
- Interest rate fluctuation
- Inflation

Economic

Technical

- Production methods
- Standards

Political

Social

- Policy changes
- Conflict
- Taxation
- Instability
- Regulation

- Buying pattern shifts
- Sudden change in consume behavior

Internal

- Loss of major client
- Sales decline

Economic

Technical

- Obsolete technology
- Change of standards

Political

Social

- Management change
- Policy changes

- Culture change
- Internal conflict

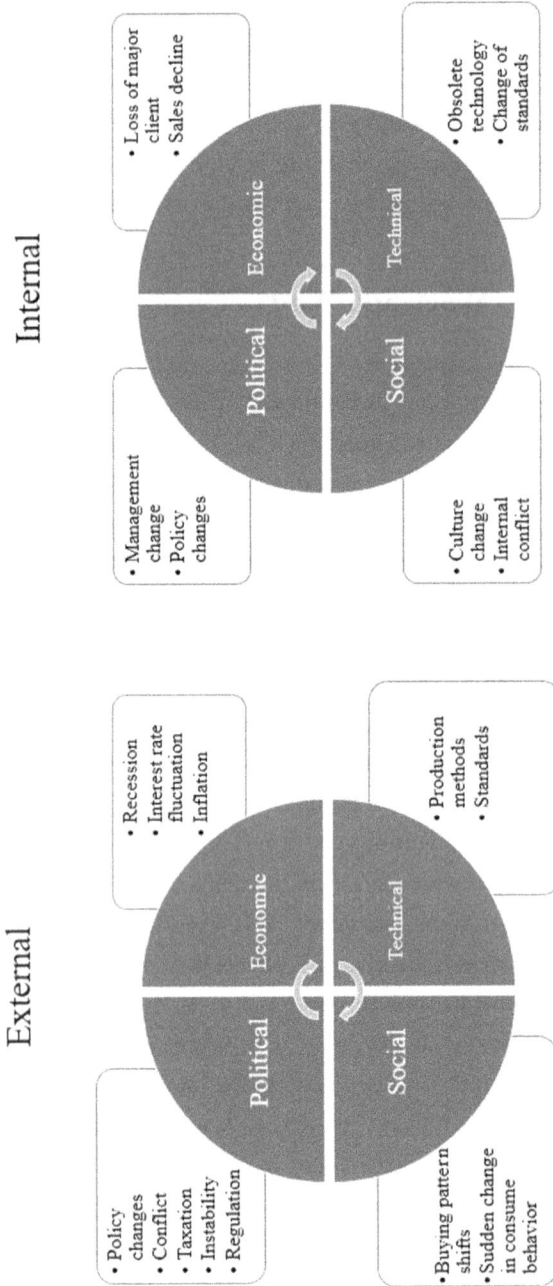

Figure 2.2 Change and change triggers

It could be suggested that change management is not something that should be limited to the response to a trigger. A company that practices continuous improvement is an example of change carried out as a response to a crisis, but to improve systems before the crisis occurs. Companies that are able to implement such ongoing change are likely to become familiar with the process and less prone to view the change with fear triggered by the uncertainty of change. Further, embarking upon change when the company is doing well tends to tap into the energy and positive morale of the employees as well as the funding made available from strong sales. Should leaders initiate change management efforts when triggered by an event or serious situation? The answer is likely to be "yes." On the other hand, is it preferred to implement an ongoing change management process to harness the efforts and resources of the organization when it is at its best? The answer also is "yes." To make a crude analogy, when the Titanic was sinking, this was not the ideal time to change the décor in the dining rooms or to rearrange the deck chairs. Such decisions, including the appropriate number of lifeboats, were best made before leaving port, and especially prior to hitting the iceberg.

PART II

The Path to Failure

Introduction to Part II: Why Learn How to Fail?

Change is complicated and difficult. Very few leaders succeed in consistently leading organizations from a low level of performance to a new state of operational excellence. Many books are written on the subject of change from nearly every angle of "how to." Leaders read such books or book summaries, yet the change they envision and seek to implement fails to materialize. One way to learn how to lead change is to study the guidelines for how to do it. Another approach is to focus on the stories of failed change attempts. Most who are exposed to such stories smile and consider how similar they are to failed events that occurred in their own companies, perhaps many times. Further, out of exposure to the cases of failed change comes the realization that "some things never change," particularly mistakes made in leading and managing change. Therefore, a leader who seeks to learn how to succeed in changing a company may do well to start with studying those who went before, who tried, and who failed, oftentimes spectacularly. The examples presented in the book offers the message that "to learn how to succeed, one must learn how to fail"—in this case, in change management.

CHAPTER 3

Failure as a Lack of Understanding

A study of common sense approaches to change as well as popular methods from the thought leaders of change management informs managers regarding what should be done, what elements should be known, and finally whom to include in change—all in the effort to minimize risk and maximize the possibility of success. History informs us, however, that change management in practice does not often go well, even when change management frameworks are employed. History also provides endless examples of change efforts that failed not only because known methods were ignored, but serious mistakes were made as well. Such mistakes in change management are more common than one might think. The study of change management mistakes therefore offers clear guidelines for certain change management failure, or stated differently, provide a guide for failure at change management. Having a working knowledge of historical mistakes in change management and then proceeding to do the opposite in practice avoids the certainty of failure and offers the opportunity of successful change. What then should change managers do if they want a guarantee of failure (or avoid so that the possibility exists for success)? To follow there are several examples with accompanying interesting stories. The names of the companies are not revealed. It is of interest to observe that each of these change failures could occur even in cases where a clear process is followed.

Failing to Understand What Needs to Be Changed

There is the old saying that "if all you have is a hammer, all of the world's problems begin to look like nails." This saying was applicable to the many global Japanese companies in the late 1990s and early 2000s who sought to compete in the global wireless telecommunications market. Today, no such companies supply products outside of the home country, but from the early 1980s to the end of the 20th century, the story of these players involved repeated attempts at market entry, exiting, trying once more, and finally giving up. Each attempt featured novel attempts at changing the formula in some way in the hopes of gaining traction in the market. Most proposed success formulas introduced by Japanese companies involved two major thrusts: tighter control by the home office and constant focus on cost reduction. The problem with these ideas is not they are bad ideas, but that they were simply not the core issues at the heart of the problem. *Newsweek* in 2008 (Caryl, 2008) made a keen observation on what Japanese companies would need to change in order to be successful in the global smartphone industry. Japanese companies traditionally experienced great success at incremental continuous improvement and cost control. However, products such as the iPhone evolved from a completely different mindset. For example, Japanese companies traditionally succeeded by taking vertical control of all products produced from components to the final delivered goods. All interaction between functions, such as engineering, marketing, and manufacturing, were managed internally within a single culture. By way of contrast, the iPhone illustrated a dramatically different way of doing business. The Apple business model, unlike the Japanese, was completely horizontal rather than vertical. Apple functioned as the lead in a massive system integration involving multiple companies and functions, widespread geography, and different cultures. Such innovative products required intensive communication and business savvy, which the Japanese companies not only were unable to do, but were unable to imagine as well. As a result, attempts at recovering the global smartphone business failed because of a failure to understand what needed to be changed (Figure 3.1).

The failure to understand what needs to change in an organization can also take place, and often does at the microscopic level. Consider, for example, a general manager who has an operation with one department that is continually underperforming. A cursory evaluation of the situation seems to indicate that the team lacks motivation and energy. Milestones are continually missed without a clear explanation for the delay.

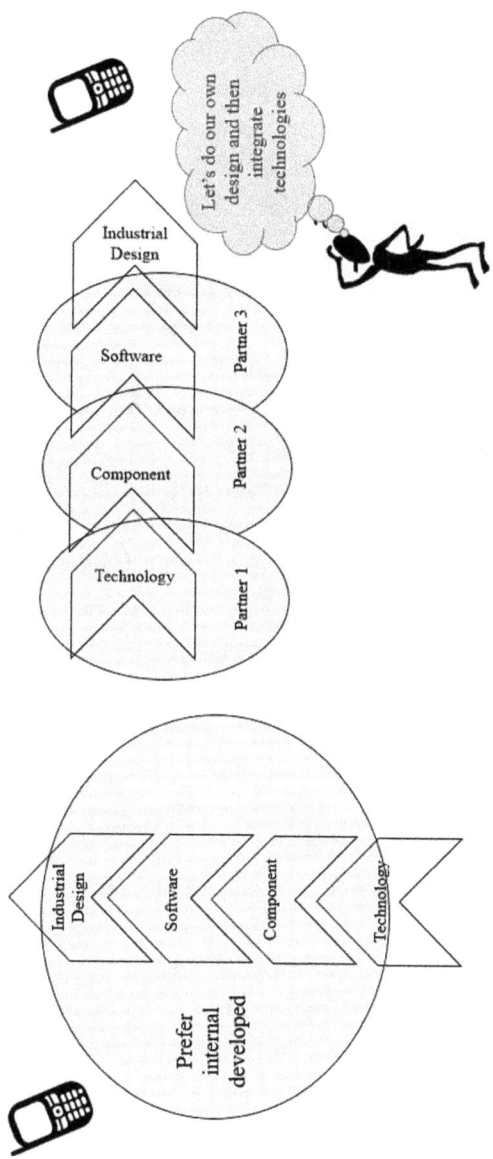

Figure 3.1 Horizontal versus vertical product development

What change is needed to ramp up the performance level of the group? Putting "two and two" together would suggest that leadership is what is lacking and therefore replacing the leader with one who is charismatic and is an excellent communicator. The general manager has just the right person in mind—a good friend in the organization who has long lobbied for a promotion. Further, the general manager made the decision to give the friend his chance, without consulting the rest of the company management team. The current leader of the group is therefore replaced with the charismatic friend of the general manager. The general manager announces the change and waits for the magic to happen and see success achieved within the department for the first time. The senior management team shook their respective heads in astonishment at the choice of replacement for the previous manager. The phrase "why didn't you run this by me first?" was heard repeatedly in the office of the GM—and of course—the watercooler. Unfortunately, the expected success never arrives, and 3 weeks later, the charismatic new leader of the group is removed. What went wrong? The general manager failed to understand that the leadership problem in the department was not one of form but of substance. What the department needed was a leader who could inspire confidence due to the depth of his technical knowledge. The charismatic new leader was able to "talk the talk" but could not "walk the walk." The team wanted a leader they could go to for answers and direction—not a motivational speaker. The performance of the department decreased rather than increase and the department employees were in a state of revolt until the new leader was removed.

What specifically needs changing within the organization may also become lost in the debate between "form" and "substance." These arguments are known to be common in the world of high technology, but the roots of this debate go further back in time. Consider for instance the old canned tuna commercial where it was argued that the public did not want "tunas with good taste," but rather "tunas that taste good." This is a form of the perennial argument of "technology versus marketing" as two contrasting approaches for how to approach positive change. It is of interest to observe that the marketing versus technology battle that substitutes for truly understanding what needs to change is fought between former marketing and technology executives. Both tend to view the world through the lens of their personal background. Such a view is likely to obscure the fact that a mix of both approaches—or neither approach—may well make for a better change solution.

Pointers for how to fail:

1. Perform a surface analysis of problems faced by the company.
2. Adopt a narrow viewpoint while thinking "inside the box."
3. Assume that the application of your traditional strengths and know-how will solve the problem.
4. Assume that leadership skills are a cure-all for organizational problems.
5. Make a strategic personnel decision without seeking counsel first.
6. Propose only change initiatives that are aligned with your functional background.

Solving the Wrong Problem

"Our company is no longer considered to be leading edge—and the existing company logo reinforces this image.... It is outdated and has the look and feel of a company 20 years ago." This observation made by a CEO of a technology company led to an intensive consultant-led effort to develop a new logo and tagline. The final logo candidates for consideration were introduced at a company retreat at which point the executive management team voted on the final selection. A few short years later, in spite of the fashionable new logo and tagline, the company went out of business. This example illustrates how a company can go wrong by doing a great job of solving the wrong problem. In the example of the "new logo design," the logo was apparently not the cause of the company's failure in the market. But, what was the real problem that needed to be solved? Was an outdated logo the root cause of declining sales and profitability? The evidence suggests that it was not. What then went wrong? The rapidly changing macroenvironment along with the ongoing clash of worldviews between executives, marketing, operations, and engineering personnel make tracing the poor business results to an associated root cause a supreme challenge. Each function in the company views the world through a different lens. The engineering function is likely to view the lack of competitiveness as a failure to spend adequate funding on product development thereby leading to products that are no longer competitive. Executives are likely to view the engineering understanding as "wrong-headed." The executive may have benchmarked current company R&D spending against competitors and already drawn the conclusion that too much is being spent on R&D. Likewise, marketing is concerned that the real problem is a failure to "get the word out" and that the message being sent to customers has gone stale. Operations managers insist that the way forward is improved efficiency. Executives seeking improvement in business have many potential "traps" into which they can fall leading to a major effort to solve a problem that in the big scheme of things does not matter. It pays to be wary of apparently simple solutions that are based more on perception and pet ideas rather than evidence (Figure 3.2).

Figure 3.2 Solving the wrong problem

The example of changing the company logo as an effort to improve business by changing the image presented by the company is but one classic example of solving the wrong problem. Another such example is the eternal problem of inventory management. Companies have long known to struggle with either not enough or too much inventory, leading to either lost customers or lost profits. This situation often exists in high-tech companies that rely on parts, subassemblies and even products shipped from distant locations. Such a company will typically be staffed with many engineering and marketing personnel involved in developing and launching products.

Personnel with this background will continually be faced with inventory problems, but will not necessarily understand what is causing them. There is a temptation for engineers or marketing personnel to say things such as "If I were in charge of inventory—things would be different." History provides examples of companies who actually listened to a vocal employee with a non-operations/inventory management background chomping at the bit to take over inventory management and fix it. Deming, one of the founders of quality management, informs managers that when problems are observed in the company, 85 percent of the time the problem is related to systems, processes, and policies. Good people tend to perform poorly when they are placed in a system that is not capable of producing good results. However, it is easier for executives to change people rather than make the effort required to improve deeply embedded intangibles such as processes, procedures, policies, and structure. The hard experience of companies who listened to a vocal employee from a different functional discipline and placed him in charge of a complex function such as inventory management is one of failure.

Attempting to solve a problem like inventory management by replacing management with a vocal employee who lacks requisite know-how is but one way to fail in change management.

Another example involves bringing in outside consultants to help a company understand why the company is has too much, not enough, or the wrong kind of inventory along with insufficient inventory turns. The interviews and training sessions between consultants and operations and material control employees appeared to be a classic example of how to initiate and lead change management. What could go wrong? Uncritical acceptance of the proposed solutions from the consultants. After a few days on site, the consultants discovered to their chagrin that the inventory and profitability problem must be related to the fact that material control was responsible for forecasting and entering orders to suppliers so that production could fill orders according to forecast. According to the consultants,

> Sales and marketing are responsible for placing demand on the factory. Sales and marketing should therefore provide the forecast to material control, and material control will implement since it is the factory and operations that are responsible for supply—in order to respond to demand presented by sales and marketing.

The problem, it would appear, was solved. However, the wrong problem was solved. When sales and marketing took over the responsibility for the forecast, the inventory ballooned out of control. The problem of insufficient inventory was mitigated, but at great expense. After a few months of growing problems, the material control and operations department started ignoring the input from sales and applied time series methods. The inventory control problem improved in that it was no worse than it was pre-consultant level. However, management came to the realization that inventory is something that will never be exactly right—so no more changes.

It is also common for executives to focus first on senior managers and attempt to implement change initiatives and improvements to the company by bringing together senior managers for a leadership retreat. Retreats such as these involve team-building events and "rah-rah" sessions in which senior managers hear presentation after presentation on the latest and greatest initiatives and new products being introduced by the company. The goal of retreats like this are to get company leaders excited and motivated about the company and its strategic direction. The good thing about these meetings is that they do tend to increase the excitement level of senior managers in the company. However, the excitement and the high energy level fades upon the return of managers to their respective offices. Why? Because once the "rah-rah" is over, it becomes clear that it is "business as usual." The announced new products are eventually launched—though typically late—while the newly announced management initiatives never seem to fully materialize. Further, the emotion and excitement also tend to drain away when it is discovered that the methodology and framework used to organize the retreat was based on a recent popular book. While the rank and file employees feel that they are engaged in evaluating problems and performing in depth analysis to provide solutions, they now discover that their executives have failed to scratch the surface of the issues and have done little more than buy a popular paperback. The problem in this is not the lack of motivation—that no popular paperback could solve in any case. The problem is that the company needs to perform better by launching new products on time and following through on the many new management and new process initiatives required for improved performance. The problem is one of execution, and raising the excitement and energy level of executives is but a marginal initial step in turning around the company. To make an analogy, it is one thing to pick up a bat and step up to the plate, but quite another to swing, connect with the ball, and successfully arrive at one or more bases. The right problem for focus is on performance and execution. The wrong problem is focusing on the emotional state of senior managers.

Pointers for how to fail:

1. Make causal connections that aren't there.
2. Uncritically accept the judgment of consultants.
3. Assume that an expert in one field can contribute expert work in a completely different field (especially when the expert is an engineer).
4. Address process and execution problems by cheering on management staff.

CHAPTER 4

Mistaken Perceptions

Solving a Perceived Rather Than a Real Problem

"We need to implement situational leadership right away," said a member of the executive team while plopping down a series of articles from academic journals on the desk of the general manager. "Morale is suffering. Turnover is high. What we have is a failure of leadership and we need to fix it!" Advice from academics and textbooks for how to run a business is endless. Thousands of different theoretical lenses, tools and techniques, and methodologies exist for how to lead and motivate people, how to implement strategy, or how to get things done. In some ways, academic theory for business is like a dinner buffet. There is plenty to eat, but it is the application of individual judgment that leads to the selection of elements that go together well as a meal. The purpose of theories, tools, and practices is to solve problems, but if the identified problem is perceived rather than real, such tools are bound to fail. In the case of morale and turnover, it is easy to jump to the conclusion that the style of leadership employed lies at the heart of the issue. But jumping to that conclusion ignores an infinity of other possible issues such as the strategy of the company, the culture, the workload, to name just a few. The rush to solve a perceived problem leads inevitably to solving the perceived problem rather than the real one, with the consequences of living with sustained ongoing turnover and moral issues (Figure 4.1).

Similar cases of solving a perceived problem are observed when a company grows from a national, to multinational, to a company with global reach. On achieving a significant level of global expansion, it is not uncommon to hear comments from executives in the home country make comments such as, "To be a global company—we must have local operations run by local managers." The perceived problem is that the lack

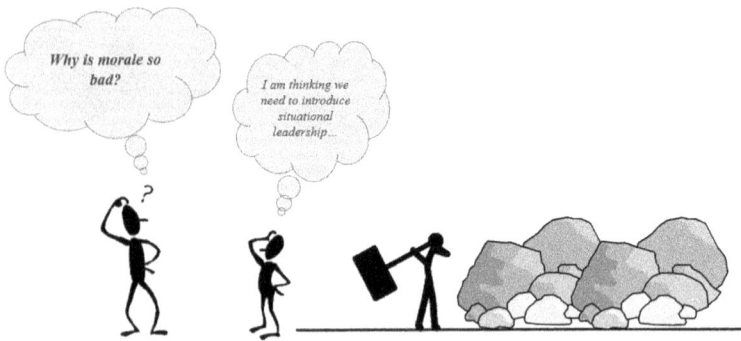

Figure 4.1 Solving a perceived rather than a real problem

of in-country local managers is somehow preventing the global company from achieving a complete level of global competence. There may be an element of truth in this perception; however, installing local managers without changes in process, decision-making, and culture lead to a company that operates much the same way as it did without local general managers. The perceived problem is "a lack of global mindset due to the lack of local management," when the actual problem is "a lack of global systems, processes, and culture that in turn lead to a lack of a 'global mindset'." Solving the perceived problem leaves the actual problem in place and perhaps makes it worse.

Financial controls can be a touchy area in any company and the opportunity for perceived problems to be solved is widespread. A typical example involves the policy associated with who has the authority to approve an expense. In one case within a multinational company, the general manager suggests that after an annual budget is approved, then the local directors of each function should have sign-off authority for their individual budgets. The rationale is that the overall budget is pre-approved, pushing sign-off authority down to directors rather than the GM correspondingly matches authority with responsibility. The perception of this proposal by corporate executives in the home country was highly negative. To address the perceived problem of the lack of financial control, executives insisted that the general manager sign-off on all expenditures. The solution to the perceived problem of a lack of control led naturally to unintended consequences. Once functional directors realized that they had no authority to approve anything, then they proceeded to send their purchase requisition "wish lists" to the general manager for negotiation and approval by the home office. Steps taken to address the perception of the lack of control led to a lack of control.

A final example of a company doing its best to solve a perceived problem is observed when executives perceive that the company salespeople are "making too much money," and in an effort to solve the perceived problem, cuts sales commissions or transfers salespeople from commission-based compensation to a salary. In one sense this action does tend to solve the problem of salespeople making too much money, but it also results in the company not making much money either. The result is observed to often not to end well in business-to-business sales contexts, but it has also taken its toll in the retail environment. For example, Circuit City switched from a commission model to hourly pay structure that is cited as one of several factors that led to the collapse of the company a year later. This is not to say that shifting from commission-based compensation to salary-based pay is always a bad idea. In many cases, this is known to be successful when the problem to be solved is the need for more account management and less pure sales and new business development. The key in such change is understanding what the needed change is and ensuring that the problem it seeks to solve is real rather than perceived.

Pointers for how to fail:

1. Apply a management theory or practice because it is promoted by a notable academic.
2. Create the appearance of a company a successful global company rather than actually be one.
3. Take steps to achieve the illusion of control rather than actual control.
4. Take steps to address an issue that bothers you, and in doing so, reduce the effectiveness of the company.

The Wrong Solution for the Right Problem

There is the old saying, "stepping over a dollar to get to a nickel." This is exactly what happens within companies that spend millions on wasted effort while at the same time, initiating vigorous internal cost-cutting measures. One such program by a multinational company was the internal "Cost Busters" program. The program sought to reduce costs on every front with emphasis on the small things such as office supplies. This effort did not seem meaningful to many given that the company had recently canceled a multimillion-dollar project that never reached the market, signed equally large contracts with external vendors without incorporating clear deliverables, and wasting significant money by ongoing delays in decision-making. Complaints to management led to responses such as "collect enough dust and it eventually becomes a mountain." Perhaps true, but with mountains of cash going out the door while the dust of cost savings was secured, the company seemed to be focused on the wrong solution for a legitimate problem. Perhaps a new saying should be coined, such as "collect enough mountains and it eventually becomes a continent." "Mountains" in the case of many dust-collecting companies involve a lack of process discipline and inefficient product development processes. Examples of this are often cited by organizations such as the Product Development Management Association. Companies lacking a structured product development and innovation and portfolio management decision-making systems are known to spend significant money on development efforts that never reach the marketplace. Counting paper clips, that is, "dust", is clearly the wrong solution for a legitimate cost problem (Figure 4.2).

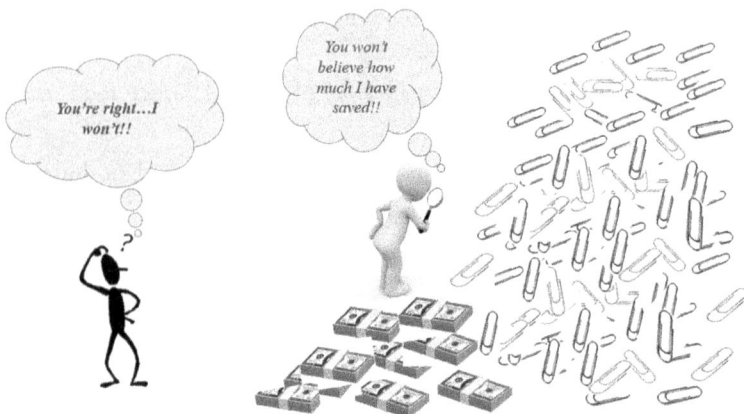

Figure 4.2 The wrong solution for the right problem

Applying the wrong solution to a clear problem may also appear in companies who acquire other companies to obtain expertise, but then proceed to "manage out" the acquired expertise by employing policies that limit the ability of the acquired company to succeed. For example, consider "Company A" with an expertise in software, networking, and switch technologies acquiring "Company B" with radio frequency technology expertise in order to compete in the market with a complete wireless system solution. The acquisition of Company B solves the problem of the lack of radio frequency design expertise in the parent company. On the other hand, Company B is also known to be limited in output capacity and is slow to introduce new products to market. Company A purchases Company B and determines that it needs to make improvements to Company B in the course of integrating the company into the new organization. What problems did Company B bring to the acquisition? Primarily a lack of efficiency, capacity, and concerns over the time to market of new products. What solution does Company A bring to the table to solve this? Company A steps in and forces Company B to incorporate its pet internal technology into its new radio frequency products. The technology does nothing to address the perceived problems of the company and is resisted by experienced engineers who are informed by public research that the favored Company A technology does not work as promised. After years of struggle against the enforcement of poor technology choices by the parent company, most of the expertise in Company B leaves and eventually the company fails and goes out of business. The lesson for change by acquisition in order to acquire expertise is to seek to solve the problems for which expertise exists, and let the acquired expertise do the job for which it was purchased. The acquired company did include some obvious shortcomings. The right solution would be to address the shortcomings rather than to insist on wrong solutions.

A final example of applying the wrong solution to the right problem is addressing client requirements in the product development process. A classic example of applying the wrong solution is a company that cancels an in-progress product development because a client, after being shown a prototype, insists that the product is not needed. Instead, the client points to an existing product from a competitor and states, "Now this is what we need!" Six months after the product development is cancelled, a major competitor launches a product similar to the one that was recently cancelled. The market shifts to the new type of product and the company restarts the cancelled product development effort. The product is eventually launched but is late to market. The problem in this case was a failure to understand product requirements, and attempting to solve it by doing exactly what the client requests and cancelling a development already underway. The supreme difficulty associated with requirements elicitation is the vetting of what a client could articulate. There is a difference between what the client says and what the client needs. In this case, the client must have needed the planned new product since shortly after the competitor launched the product, the competitor shifted to the new technology. It is easy to do exactly what the customer says, which is the wrong solution to the right problem—in this case, requirements elicitation. It is far more difficult to understand what the client needs and to understand what underlying drivers that will lead the client to ultimately select one type of product versus another. The wrong solution to the right problem is often an "easy" solution that lacks thoughtful analysis of the problem.

Pointers for how to fail:

1. Solve small problems when you are not able to solve large ones.
2. Actively snuff out the expertise of a company that was acquired for its expertise.
3. Always do exactly what clients tell you to do.

CHAPTER 5

Failed Transplants

Transplanting a Change Solution from Another Company

It is common for companies embarking on change to bring in new management from the outside. When this happens, the new leadership may tend to do "what comes natural." This usually involves carrying out the policies that were used in a previous company. Sometimes the policy "transplants" work, but often they do not. Consider the case of a telecommunications company bringing in a new executive to turn around the company and foster a more performance-driven culture. It was noted by the board that the company lacked an incentive plan that focused the energies of all employees to consistently deliver projects on time. The lack of an incentive plan was perceived to be the cause of the ongoing poor project schedule performance. The new executive knows exactly what to do, and that is to implement the bonus plan used in the previous company. The company from which the executive came implemented a bonus structure that was also said to have been taken from GE by the executive who joined the previous company from GE. The bonus structure used in the previous company was tiered so that the bonus percentage increased based on the rank of the employee. Rank and file employees received 5 to 10 percent, and the percentage increased to approximately 40 percent for the most senior executive. The company that used this bonus scheme was a rapidly growing publicly traded company, and all employees were aware of the overall bonus percentages awarded. It was understood by those who sought out higher bonus levels that the path to bonus prosperity involved promotion to management (Figure 5.1).

The bonus plan was introduced by the executive to the new company in an all-hands meeting. It was expected that the employees would be overjoyed to have a bonus plan given that they had never had one before. The

Figure 5.1 Failed transplants

response to the plan was instantaneous, and highly negative. In fact, at least one employee engaged in a red-faced angry screaming session in the office of the executive. Why the negative result? The new executive presenting the plan failed to understand the collectivist culture of the company associated with its long history as a satellite operation of a company with roots in Japan. The negative reaction was not related to the bonus per se, but rather that the bonus levels were tiered by rank. This was a bonus scheme that worked well in a Western high-tech growth company, but not in a company with a long history of immersion in an egalitarian culture that exalted the role of teamwork and the philosophy of "we are all in this together."

Bonus schemes are not the only "transplants" that fail to achieve what is promised in a change management effort. New executives tend to also be familiar with the organizational structure of their previous home. Such a structure may or may not be compatible with the objectives and the business operation of the new company, yet new executives sometimes implement a new structure without a deep understanding of what is or is not likely to work well in the new environment. A typical example is of an executive who makes a comment such as "We never had these management levels in the previous company—so I am going to eliminate the one management level we did not use where I worked before." A comment such as this may seem reasonable on the surface, but it does depend on what the work of the new organization really is. Also, this comment should lead to reflection upon management levels used within organizations and why they are needed in the first place. Senior managers are observed to focus on strategic matters, for example, determining what businesses the company should be as well as what actions the company should carry out in order to achieve financial and market-share goals. Lower level managers and individual contributors tend to focus on executing the strategy that emanates from the top of the organization. The lower the level of the organization, the more the focus on performing work and addressing day-to-day issues. In contrast, the higher the level in the organization, the more that the focus is on "where we are going and why." In the case of the "we don't need this management level" executive, flattening the organization to make senior managers "do it all" produced unintended consequences. The senior managers who once sought to lead and direct their respective groups, now, on losing a lower level of management, began to get dragged down into the day-to-day issues of the organization. The new leader failed to recognize the difference in context as well as the workload differences between the previous company and the new company. Cost savings were apparent in the removal of a management level, with the consequence that groups formerly led by senior managers who focused on decision-making and direction-setting were now led by senior managers who "did a little bit of everything" except set direction. The result was rather like a car going on a trip without a map, compass, or destination, while achieving excellent fuel economy in the process.

Another case of a transplant involves executives who adopt a process or methodology originally adopted in a completely different operational context. The executive may have used the methodology in previous engagements and understand how to use it perfectly in the old operational environment. However, when transplanted to the new context, the implementation is unclear, and the result is not successful. It is not the case that the transplanted idea could never work, but it could only work with an appropriate understanding of how to use it in the new context. Some examples include:

Statistical process control. A methodology associated with manufacturing that involves tracking long runs of data to assess whether the process is in or out of control. When transplanted into a context that does not produce long runs of data and the process to be controlled is unclear, the transplanted methodology breaks down (e.g., the application of statistical process control in a project environment or other one-time-only activity).

Assembly lines. A successful methodology that produces continuous output with consistent quality that is ideal for repetitive component placement and specification setting. When transplanted to an environment where every assigned job is unique and challenging, the methodology breaks down (e.g., the application of the assembly-line methodology to a repair depot where every repair requires extensive troubleshooting and a variety of different solutions).

Self-managed teams. Self-managed teams are ideal in cell manufacturing settings where the nature of the work is unambiguous and the context is highly structured. Implementing this scheme in an ambiguous and unstructured setting may lead to teams that tend to veer from the strategic alignment of the company. On the other hand, implementing self-managed teams within a framework such as Agile may work given that Agile management guidelines foster team self-management. In the absence of a well-thought-out management scheme, transplanted self-management teams may founder (Figure 5.2).

Figure 5.2 More failed transplants

Pointers for how to fail:

1. Introduce a compensation scheme from a company operating in a different context, culture, industry, or all of the above.
2. Eliminate management layers to emulate a previous company operating in a different context, culture, industry, or all of the above.
3. Insist that senior managers keep busy with operational tasks rather than strategic decision-making.
4. Transplant a process or methodology from a familiar to an alien context.

CHAPTER 6

Goal-Setting Problems

SMART versus DUMB Goals

How motivating is it when an executive is speaking in front of an organization and says something like, "We need to leverage cross-functional core competencies"? What does this mean? Who knows? A guideline for an effective change manager is to speak in such a way that when the speech is over, the members in the audience can then exit the room knowing exactly what actions to take that could contribute to the top-level strategy of the company. This is the rationale behind SMART goals. SMART refers to Specific, Measurable, Attainable, Relevant, and Time-Bound. An example of a smart goal for a change initiative is:

> We will increase sales of product "A" (specific) by 5% (measurable) using our 2 new salespeople (attainable) to increase revenues (relevant) during the next fiscal year (time-bound).

In contrast to SMART goals, DUMB goals are Dubious, Unclear, Misguided, and Belated. Stated differently, such goals are questionable, they are "fuzzy," they are based on faulty assumptions, and they are presented too late to be useful. DUMB goals abound in the business world today, and the acronym of goal failure may be explored one letter at a time, as follows:

"D" Is for Dubious

A dubious goal is one that is proposed that is out of character for a company, beyond the capabilities of the company, or otherwise questionable for several reasons. A typical dubious goal in the context of change management is announcing that the company is going to offer a new service for which the company has no experience. Further, the company announcing it has never offered services previously and fails to understand the implications of offering a service to other parts of the business. While it is natural for manufacturing and product-based companies to seek to improve margins by offering services, such a strategy is not without dangers. For example, consider a manufacturer who manufactures, sells, and installs wireless telecommunications equipment. It is observed by senior management that customers installing the equipment also install satellite communications equipment to aid in offering nationwide services. For senior managers, this appears to be a service for which a competitor is getting a "piece of the pie" that could otherwise go to them. A partnership was established with a satellite manufacturing and service company and the company got into the business of offering satellite services and installing them at the time of installation of the system sale. The opportunity offered not only more revenue, but recurring revenue. What could go wrong? The aspect of offering such a service that made it a dubious prospect was the fact that when a satellite service was disrupted in any way, the entire communications system, whether regional or national, would go offline. This situation would impact hundreds of thousands of customers who relied on the service. Given that the manufacturing company was not experienced at offering a real-time service that must never "go down," the system did go down and it did so many times. What was the impact to the business? Affected customers demanded compensation, or withheld purchases or payment on previous equipment purchases. The dubious service offering was eventually scrapped as it took more time and effort than warranted, and proved very costly due to the ongoing mistakes.

Examples of the dubious goal existing outside of telecommunications. A company that manufactures heavy equipment seeks to improve its overall profitability by offering repair and equipment refurbishing services. Customers who bought new equipment could now also buy equipment refurbished from customer trade-ins. Also, customers purchasing new and refurbished equipment could send in equipment for repair, rent equipment, or purchase parts. These services offer the potential for increasing the interaction of the customer with the manufacturer throughout the lifecycle of the product. As well, service revenue could supplement revenue from equipment sales and, in addition, provide additional revenues when new equipment sales slowed. The concept of offering such services paints a beautiful picture, albeit one that is dubious. Reasons for the questionable nature of the goal could be observed shortly after the new service was launched. Clients who sent in equipment for repair or refurbish could claim that they were not satisfied with the service, dispute the bill, and withhold orders for new equipment while the dispute continued. Such leverage by clients often led to a positive outcome for the client, and a negative one for the manufacturer. To make things worse, the clients who were offered these services began to see the manufacturer as "moving in on my territory." After all, clients of the heavy equipment manufacturer also repaired, refurbished, and rented equipment, in addition to selling parts. The backlash against the service grew, and the questionable plan to increase revenues using this service was eventually scrapped.

"U" Is for Unclear

"Tomorrow we will start knowledge management in this company." Who upon hearing this directive from a senior executive would be prepared to act? How would change unfold from such direction? The answer is, "it depends." The term "knowledge management" means different things to different people. Part of the reason for this is that knowledge management is a kind of management "buzzword" that is often used loosely in senior executive conversations and speeches. It is used loosely because knowledge management is not a "thing," rather, it is many things, such as systems, processes, policies, and implementation steps. The general idea behind a concept such as knowledge management is that the knowledge that resides in the mind of employees could be extracted, documented, stored, retrieved, and institutionalized. Knowledge management is therefore an emergent phenomenon that unfolds after many different actions are taken over a period of time. There is the old saying, "He who knows, does not say. He who says, does not know." Given that knowledge management is an example of an emergent construct, an executive who speaks of it in a simple manner is very likely not one who understands the implications of the directive. At minimum, the directive to implement an emergent construct is an example of an unclear goal.

The term "portfolio management" is another example of an unclear directive. An executive concerned about the profitability of product lines and the cost of product development may issue a directive to implement portfolio management as the basic policy underlying a proposed change in direction. The trouble with such a directive is that the term is not clear. Portfolio management can refer to the management of a bundle of financial holdings, but in this case, it is referring to product development and project management decision-making. How then would the concept of portfolio management be implemented? It depends on how it is understood by those tasked with implementing it. In practice, the term, like the term "knowledge management," is used loosely and generally refers to various policies, procedures, and milestones for deciding what product development projects to fund, which to cancel, which to emphasize more, and which to deemphasize. In general, the directive to act upon a construct that refers to a significant number of underlying activities is an unclear directive or goal and should be avoided.

Unclear goals in change management also include those that create organizational structures that lack enough detail for their operation. An example of this includes a product design group that came to the realization that the procurement of parts, labor, and software applications included both business and technical management concerns. On the one hand, achieving the lowest cost possible is a typical business goal of a purchasing group. Realizing this goal often requires that the final vendor selection be delayed for as long as possible so that many players compete against each other so that the price is reduced. On the other hand, engineering is motivated to select the vendor as soon as possible so that design work may begin immediately. Senior executives seeing the need to closely manage such process seek to change the purchasing process and does so by establishing two procurement groups, one in engineering and one in business operations to ensure that both sets of issues are addressed. The new organization is announced, and the problems begin. Why? Although a new organization was established, the directive to establish the new organization was unclear due to the lack of detail regarding how it should operate. For example, the scope of responsibility and authority was not clearly defined, and neither were the boundaries of each organization.

Further, it was unclear which purchasing group, if any, had the final authority to make the final vendor selection and announce it to the vendor. The lack of clarity regarding how the new organization was supposed to work together led to intense conflict. The conflict became even more significant after the ongoing anxiety and problems were raised to the senior executive level who added even less clarity by stating "you guys just work it out."

"M" Is for Misguided

The CEO of a company steps up to the microphone on stage and kicks off the annual all-hands meeting that the goal of the company is to achieve a 10 percent share of the global market. The achievement of such a goal would be stunning, particularly given that the company currently has far less than one-tenth of 1 percent of global market share. Presenting a stretch goal as a means for revitalizing the company is a reasonable idea. However, a directive that "stretches" too far, too fast could be said to be misguided. There is the old saying, "bend, but not break." A misguided stretch goal may in fact "break."

Misguided goals do not have to be big stretch goals to be misguided. In fact, apparently small goals may carry the company off-course for many reasons. An example of an apparently small goal is a CEO who states that "... the global market for this product is one billion units annually ... and if we achieve only 1% of this market, we will all be rich!" The one percent figure would appear to be a relatively small and achievable goal. However, it is not for a company who currently holds less than 1/10,000 of one percent of the global market. The apparently small goal is misguided for two reasons:

1. The apparently small goal is actually a very large goal that is likely unattainable.
2. Large markets attract significant competition whereby profitability often gets competed away.

Another old saying is that "niches have riches." Unlike a small underserved market, a very large market for which one company is attracted may be appealing to many players. The resulting competition makes capturing a piece of the pie quite difficult, particularly for small existing players who are not well established in the marketplace. In addition, the established players with existing large market share will very likely implement strong barriers to entry for newcomers by making it easy for existing customers to keep buying from legacy suppliers thereby keeping switching costs high.

Finally, it is also misguided to seek to change the company by promoting a move into a new market with a new product. The least risky ventures are those involving existing products and existing markets. The difficulty and risk associated with entering new markets with new products are easily underestimated. There is the old saying that "the less the company knows about something ... the more attractive it appears to be." One case in point may involve a company who manufactures engines and hydraulics making the decision to enter the heavy equipment business within the construction industry. After all, such an industry uses the components currently manufactured by the existing company. How difficult could it be to take the components currently being developed and manufactured? All it would take is to encase existing components with steel, bucket loading devices, and wheels. What is wrong with this picture? Embarking on change by making the decision to enter this new market without previous experience is misguided for many reasons. The first issue to be missed is the fact that the use of heavy equipment within the construction industry is often dangerous—safety concerns, testing, and approvals about. An accident with such equipment could easily lead to lawsuits. The second concern is the barrier to entry of newcomers. Sales of construction equipment often are made to rental companies who rent machines to construction firms. After 3 years of renting the equipment to customers, the rental companies trade in the equipment for substantial discounts on new equipment. It is often difficult and costly for newcomers to break that virtuous revenue cycle of purchase, rent, and trade-in enjoyed by customers of legacy suppliers. Further, rental companies have long-standing relationships with manufacturers. The industry does not turn on technological expertise, but rather on relationships and trust. Breaking the relationship bonds between clients and legacy suppliers is a long and winding, and expensive, road. Assuming that the industry is "ripe for the picking" because the technology is not challenging is therefore seriously misguided.

"B" Is for Belated

There is the old saying that "not making a decision … is in fact a decision." This saying may be forgotten at times by executives who are not able to make a move until all aspects of a plan are thoroughly analyzed so that "all pieces of the puzzle" appear to fit together. The endless delay in decision-making is sometimes referred to as "analysis paralysis" and is therefore a cause of delayed or belated decision-making. The problem with belated decisions is twofold. First, life does not come to a halt while the organization waits for an executive decision. The internal life of the organization as well as the events within the macroenvironment continue unabated. Second, a plan is only a plan; therefore, no matter how complete or sophisticated it may be, when the plan meets reality it will rarely go as planned. This was recognized by one of the great military planners of World War I Helmuth von Moltke who is known to have said, "No battle plan ever survives contact with the enemy." The lesson here is that a decision made too late may not only no longer be valid, but the plan associated with the decision might not work as expected anyway. History provides several categories of examples of companies who did seek to change, but the attempt came too late to make a difference. Examples include major retailers who responded too late to the rise of e-commerce, film manufacturers who waited too late to "go digital," or video rental stores who waited too late to shift to streaming services. Today's good idea for change may be tomorrow's failed attempt at becoming something better.

Don't Be DUMB

Prior to issuing a change directive, a new policy, or just a new idea, it is highly recommended that executives or change managers test the idea first to learn how DUMB. the policy is. If the policy is a stretch goal that few employees will accept, if it is so unclear that it cannot be implemented, or if it is "wrongheaded" or just too late, chances are that it is a DUMB move that is likely to lead to the failure of the proposed change (Figure 6.1).

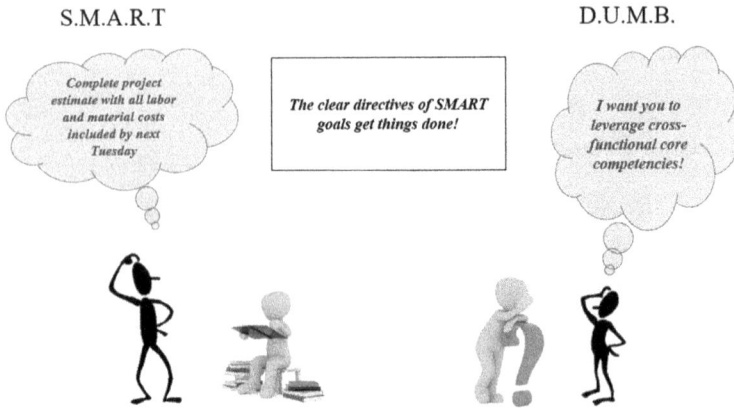

Figure 6.1 SMART versus DUMB

Pointers for how to fail:

1. Advocate for questionable, out of context change initiatives.
2. Promote the adoption of practices loosely defined by buzzwords.
3. Pursue markets because they are large.
4. Implement a new organizational design without explaining how it is supposed to work.
5. Enter a new market with a new product.
6. Analyze a change decision until the opportunity has passed.

CHAPTER 7

Grasping at "Big" Straws

Double Down on What Used to Work

Imagine a sailing ship company faced within increasing steam ship competition in the late 19th century. What steps should the company take to succeed? One solution would be to adopt the advanced steam technology and use it to increase speed and reliability of ships crossing the seven seas. Another approach would be to conduct additional research and invest in tooling to improve sails, sail placement, and hull shapes to ramp up the speed of ocean-going sailing ships. It is obvious in hindsight that the sailing-ship advancement strategy would be doomed to failure considering available new technology. While this may be true, the "doubling down on what used to work" strategy remains alive and well today.

One example of such "doubling down" involves an entire industry. In the 1980s and early 1990s, small "mom and pop" answering services and paging services were gobbled up by large investors. This activity was driven by the advent of digital paging protocols that could transform a single channel with several hundred paging subscribers to a cash cow with well over 100,000 subscribers. Small paging companies morphed into regional and nationwide paging companies. Millions of subscribers in this period encountered the wonder of typing in a number on a pay phone and have someone's beeper go off and display a number on the other side of the country. In the telecommunications environment of the 1980s and early 1990s, no wireless telecommunication service could beat the battery life, the coverage, and the efficiency of digital pagers. During this period, cellular phones were gradually shifting from analog to digital protocols. They remained expensive in terms of purchase price and monthly fees. Battery life was such that cellular phones required daily charging—for those that did use batteries rather than permanently plug into a vehicle. Pager battery life by way of contrast typically lasted approximately 1 month. Few envisioned that the cellphone industry would soon catch up and surpass what paging services could provide. However, the growth of digital cellular that included text messaging and nationwide roaming began to drive a shift in the preferences of wireless consumers. In retrospect, the mid-1990s should have signaled the beginning of the end of paging and the rise of cellular. However, instead of shifts to new technologies, many companies seemed determined to double down on what previously worked. One wireless infrastructure purchased a device company to deepen their presence in the paging industry. Others who served both the paging and the cellular industry saw a bright future in paging and continued to insist that the role of the cellular phone would remain limited. It was common to hear statements such as "people will never do Web browsing on a mobile device" and "the killer application for the cellphone beyond voice is messaging" expressing the firm belief that the success of the cellular phone was contingent upon it adopting and reinforcing those features that made paging successful. Many players in the paging industry lined up to purchase frequencies from the FCC to offer a new service referred to as "Narrowband Personal Communications Services" or NPCS. The umbrella term "NPCS" referred to the offering of two-way paging services with somewhat higher transmission speeds. Two-way paging used receivers in the field as well as transmitters. The "return channel" required for two-way operation provided the capability for pagers to respond to messages, but at the cost of a higher monthly bill and significantly reduced battery life. At the same time, cellular phones, products that offered similar but more powerful features, began to offer significantly improved size, weight, coverage, and battery life. Ultimately, paging was replaced by the far more capable digital cellular services, and two-way paging never got off the ground despite hundreds of millions of investment dollars. It seems that history repeats itself, and once again, sailing ship manufacturers continued to envision a world in which steamships could never compete (Figure 7.1).

The act of "doubling down" can occur at a smaller scale at the product level. Japanese companies, for example, are known for their expertise at making small and lightweight hardware. However, they were beaten to the world "smaller and lighter" cellular phone market with the launch

Figure 7.1 Doubling down

of the Motorola RAZR phone. Recall that Japanese companies tend to develop products from the bottom up using their own in-house components. Consider a real-life conversation between a Japanese executive and an executive from a major global wireless operator discussing the benefits of Motorola's RAZR phone.

> *Wireless Operator Executive:* "We love the RAZR phone. It is small, lightweight, and customers love it."
>
> *Japanese Executive:* "We will soon have our own small and thin product."
>
> *Wireless Operator Executive:* "Well—that's good! But we already have one now."
>
> *Japanese Executive:* "Yes, but ours will be better. (The executive holds of a poster that features an array of tiny components.) Notice how Motorola "cheated." They made their phone smaller by changing the orientation of the battery—making the phone a bit wider than it should be. Our new phone will feature all in-house developed small components!"
>
> *Wireless Operator Executive:* "So what?"

The "doubling down" phenomena in this case is to respond to global change in the product market by making small components in-house. After all, it worked in the era of the Walkman and miniaturized transistor radios and TVs. This must be the time to "double down." On an even smaller scale, "doubling down on what used to work" occurs frequently at the organizational and operational levels. Some examples observed over time include:

1. "Let's promote from within—it worked great last time we did it."
2. "Let's bring in someone from outside—it worked great last time we did it."
3. Insisting on design rules in new product development that favored a functional area that was once the dominant player in the organization.

An actual example of enforcing legacy design rules involves a factory that will approve the transfer of a design to the factory so long as specific design rules are followed. Naturally it could be expected that the design rules would benefit the factory and help them achieve improved yields and consistently meet specifications. But, what if such design rules required the use of components that could not be serviced in the field, and that the current business model required field service to be carried out for the company to be profitable? Insisting on the adoption of such design rules paid dividends in the past, but will doubling down and doing it again still make sense during a time when the company is shifting to a services-intensive business model?

To Double Down or Not?

Jim Collins in "Good to Great" refers to the "flywheel effect" as an important factor contributing to the success of the business. The flywheel effect describes how a company "sticks to their knitting" and keeps plugging away at doing what they do best until the profitability and efficiency of the company takes flight and produces results exponentially better with runaway success. It would appear the Jim Collins suggests that "doubling down" is the path to success. However, it is observed in many cases that it is not. How then should change managers think about this principle when reflecting on "doing what worked before" rather than "doing something new"? Perhaps it is preferred to avoid narrowly defining what was previously done. In the wireless communications example, perhaps the public was willing to purchase simple and cost-effective products and services when alternatives were lacking. In the case of the demise of the sailing ship as well as the paging industry, perhaps it was not "sailing ship passage" or "paging services" that clients were purchasing, but rather "oceanic transportation" and "wireless communication services." Conceptualizing a wider view of what was done in the past may lead to a successful "doubling down" of the principle of what was once executed, rather than the specific product or service.

Pointers for how to fail:

1. Do what you know how to do rather than what the market requires you to do.
2. Do exactly what you previously did that worked in another time and context, but this time only harder.
3. Narrowly define what it is that your company does to limit opportunities to evolve.
4. Fail to grasp the current means for attaining a competitive advantage in the marketplace.

GOBASH

A common saying that arose in the 1990s was "Go big or stay home," leading to the acronym GOBASH. The idea expressed in this statement was that if a company were to be successful, it must be "all in." It must ramp-up and scale-up or be left behind. This thinking was perhaps natural during the period characterized by both the telecom boom and the "dot-com bubble." However, it did lead to companies looking ahead to see a future through rose-colored glasses. This was a future with nothing but expansion, and therefore companies needed to get ready for it or risk falling behind. This thinking led to change initiatives in many companies that were focused exclusively on the expansion of capacity. One such company involved a multioperation organization that was built from several acquisitions. Two of the sites included manufacturing of different products with each manufacturing operation, each managed by separate and different business systems. The different business systems featured different processes, and the process differences for placing orders, scheduling manufacturing, and ordering material were seen to be a limiting factor given the expected increased growth in the business. The process difference between the two manufacturing facilities caused additional bottlenecks in getting the product out the door. This was because clients typically purchased products from both factories and then integrated and installed them on site. Furthermore, orders placed for both facilities were taken at a third operation thereby complicating the job of order entry. It was therefore decided in the spirit of GOBASH to replace the different systems with a single enterprise resource planning (ERP) system that would provide consistent processes between the two factories as well as the order entry operation. The projected multimillion-dollar 18-month implementation project was considered a worthy investment because it paved the way for the company to deliver according to the expected increased market demand. To add to this investment, the company considered it prudent to expand development capacity and therefore broke ground on a $20 million new facility near one of the manufacturing sites. Did "going big" pay off? The multiyear ERP implementation began as the industry peaked and, once implemented, 2 years later provided a platform to support manufacturing and sales of less than half the original volume of product. The expected volume never materialized. To make matters worse, each operation sought to make the new system function similar to the legacy system when the new system was implemented. The new, advanced, and sophisticated ERP system functioned somewhat differently in each operation and operated very similarly to the old system. Had the market grown instead of collapsing, the limitations of the legacy systems would still remain. The new system would likely have acted as more of a bottleneck than the legacy system since employees at each operation would employ their own "workarounds" to make the new system function like the old one. The ERP investment to support capacity expansion was never needed and the money wasted. The new building was soon to follow as the operation remained in the old facility and sold off the new one (Figure 7.2).

It may also be tempting to "count one's chickens before they hatch" when everyone else is counting theirs. One significant constraint on capacity to deliver in the dot-com boom was software development capability. Many high-tech companies sought software development resources in India, China, Eastern Europe, and anywhere in the world where software

Figure 7.2 ǦOBASH *with ERP*

skills could be tapped. The rush was on to gobble up software resources. One common tactic in this war for skill sets was to drop recruiters into companies that were closing and laying off staff. One large company with a telecommunications division observed this happening several times but was late to the software skill acquisition game. A company in Canada with significant software expertise announced layoffs and the telecommunications division saw a chance to catch up at last. The company hired 50 people and set up a software development center. The company continued to hire and acquired a new larger building to house the developers in preparation for developing the software that would power the next generation of product. While this was happening, sales of the most profitable product line began to decline. Concerns about the cost of continuing to try to advance market share within the global market were raised at the CEO level. What was the result? After finally getting a change to acquire an additional software team and develop it into a center of excellence, the declining market prospects forced management to take a hard look at the business with the goal in mind of changing course. Within 6 months, the brand-new software operation was shut down. Change that is proposed to address imagined future growth is a gamble. Winners of this gamble are heroes, likely because there are so few of them.

Pointers for how to fail:

1. Overestimate future sales growth.
2. Assume that a market that is growing today will continue to grow tomorrow.

3. Go big with major fixed cost investments because others are doing it.

4. Assume that an ERP system implementation will save the company.

Betting the Company on the Big Idea

A CEO from a major client visits the home country of a major manufacturer with significant operations in the United States. During this visit, the CEO observes a unique product that does not exist in the United States. The client CEO is intrigued by the product and upon returning home presents a vision to the board of directors of how this product can transform the company. The board agrees and the CEO calls for a meeting with the CEO of the sales, marketing, and manufacturing operations in the United States. After extensive discussions and negotiations between the client company, the CEO of the parent company agrees to develop a version of the product for the United States. The client ramps up a marketing campaign, customer training programs and materials, inventory capacity, and distribution capability for the new product. The manufacturer ramps up purchasing and increases component inventory and manufacturing capacity to meet the contractual requirement of 5,000 units per month for the first year. The U.S.-based operation of the manufacturer sets up alliances and partnerships to source local components and product support. It is "all systems go" for transformation upon the introduction of "the big idea." After the first two shipments of the new product, the manufacturer is hungry for news of the "sell-through" of the product from the client to end users. The client company is very quiet. Eventually, the manufacturer receives formal communication requesting that all future shipments of the new product be cancelled. Unfortunately, a large percentage of the products were already made and in inventory, while the shipments for the next 2 months were already in transit and required to be redirected. What happened? It seems that there was a reason why the product was successful outside of the United States, but not inside. The use case for the product was completely different. This understanding did not become clear until the first few weeks of sales as well as significant returns (Figure 7.3).

Countries outside the United States are not the only source of big ideas. Big ideas guaranteed to save the company often originate inside

Figure 7.3 The big idea

companies and require an internal champion to garner support for the idea. When a big idea reaches a critical mass of support, market studies are certain to follow. Skeptics of the new idea may be persuaded upon review of data from focus groups that signal the need for the new product in the market as well as the client willingness to buy. Such focus group data include videos of product demonstrations along with client reactions. Further, the positive product data can reach inches think reams of reports ready for senior management and marketing executive review. The big idea is adopted as a focus for change and transformation of the company. Significant investment follows and the product is launched accompanied with great fanfare. Then, nothing happens. The product fails and the company retrenches and is eventually acquired at a small fraction of its original valuation. What went wrong? It is one thing to have a member of a focus group offer a favorable response to a product and state that the product would be purchased at the price proposed by the focus group facilitators. It is quite another thing to have actual people in real life decide that a product has value, is worth purchasing, and results in customers taking money out of a wallet and making a purchase.

Finally, big ideas in change initiatives are not limited to product ideas. They can involve ideas for how an organization should be structured, how the workspace of all employees should be organized, or any other policy or process ideas that are in fact the pet big ideas of a senior executive who finally arrived at a position where he or she is able to pursue it. Such instances of big ideas are often promoted with the deeply seated belief that "if we only did _____, we would transform the company!" The challenge of this category of big idea is that they tend to only be "big" from the point of view of those promoting them. Some examples include:

1. "We need to get rid of cubicles and create an open office environment to facilitate communication between functions!"
2. "Going forward, all managers leading [fill in blanks] will be required to be certified in [fill in blanks]."
3. New dress codes that may or may not include ties, sports coats, jeans, no jeans, casual Fridays, Hawaiian Wednesdays, to name but a few possibilities.
4. We will reinvigorate the structure of the organization by (select all that apply):
   a. Removing levels of management
   b. Adding levels of management
   c. Implementing cross-functional teams
   d. Initiating a telecommuting program
   e. Cancelling a previously promoted telecommuting program
5. We will institute forward-looking titles for each position (e.g., chief culture officer) and insist that everyone refer to each other by their first names only.

While it is good for executives to be passionate about change and fine-tuning of the organization, one person's big idea can be another's wrong turn. It pays for executives to remember that their ideas are not special. In fact, because executives and change agents enjoy positions of power by which they can impress their ideas upon, an organization requires that such leaders pay special attention to the vetting of big ideas by a management team who has the freedom to speak up. A leadership team who "shoots down" a bad big idea has provided a service for the executive. Further, tacit agreement or positive feedback about an idea that is bad makes it no less bad. Employees who fail to speak out about a bad idea leave the room with the negative impressions swimming around and festering in their heads. A skilled change manager will encourage employees to get those concerns out on the table in hopes of together developing a better, more practical, or perhaps smaller idea.

Pointers for how to fail:

1. Readily introduce popular foreign products who use case is not fully understood.
2. Believe the following: "Runaway successes in other countries will lead to success, change, and transformation if introduced in a different country."
3. Trust rosy forecasts for the new product and prepare accordingly.
4. Uncritically accept focus group data on proposed new products.
5. Implement that pet "big idea" as soon as the opportunity presents itself.

The Savior from the Outside

Imagine the first day on the job of a new CEO brought in to save the company. There is a mixture of uneasiness as well as excitement. Those at the top of the hierarchy are naturally nervous. Those at the bottom are hopeful that things will get better. Within 30 days, several key people are fired. Within 60 days, a retinue of friends of the CEO from the last place that they all worked join the company. Within 90 days, most employees shake their heads and sigh when they hear a meeting begin with "... well this is the way WE did it." It becomes obvious at this point that members of the CEO's new team are "in," while the legacy staff are "out." Key people begin to leave and are snapped up by competitors where they are more appreciated. The savior from the outside brings in many fresh ideas, but most are not achievable given the constraints presented by the new industry, which, in fact, the new CEO knows little about. There are some bright spots in the tenure of the new executive. Several new products are launched to the marketplace that are followed by strong sales. Many press releases and press conferences follow with the CEO taking full credit for the recent successes. The new CEO of course fails to mention that the new products were initiated under the guidance of the former CEO. Eventually, the sales of the new products taper off and few truly new products' ideas and launches are forthcoming. All the "new" products that enjoy some success are updates to previous product lines. Those products that are new and the brainchild of the new CEO seem out of context for the industry and are not accepted by the market. The new CEO naturally prepared for the rosiest of market scenarios and therefore created a substantial inventory and addition fixed capacity cost problem. The board of directors after 2 years become frustrated with the new CEO, and the CEO's contract, which includes a large "golden parachute," is terminated. A legacy team member who was formerly in charge of engineering and manufacturing operations is promoted and the company is steered back to the right path. The former CEO (and his "retinue") yet again moves to a different industry and provides several public interviews about how the company from which he just "resigned" lacked creativity and was not sufficiently advanced so that his vision could be fully realized. So ends a typical tale of initiating change by bringing in the "savior from the outside" (Figure 7.4).

Figure 7.4 The savior from the outside

It is said that the most risk of product launches are when companies attempt to launch new products into new markets. The reason for this is obvious—many unknowns exists about both the product to be delivered and the market into which it is delivered. Something similar could be said about bringing in a "savior" with a background that seems sufficiently like that of the market and culture of the new company, but in fact is very different. Although a company may bring in such an executive to seed the organization with new ideas, the new ideas may be bad ideas. For example, consider a company that manufactures wireless electronic telecommunications devices sold to end users. Such a company may reach out to an executive who formerly led a consumer electronics division of another company, but not a wireless device company. A prospective "savior" may be alternatively sourced from a wireless telecommunications company that manufacturer infrastructure rather than wireless consumer devices. What are the risks associated with changing a company by bringing in apparently similar yet very different executives? For starters, consumer electronics such as TVs and consumer audio are quite different in complexity from a wireless device such as a cellular phone. The level of interaction of a cellular phone customer with the device, the layers of software and middleware, and the multiple connectivity options make smartphones orders of magnitude higher in software and systems development complexity than an apparently related (yet unrelated) product such as a TV, computer, or consumer audio device. As an example of complexity, each keystroke on a smartphone engages multiple layers of software, multiple processors, and a radio channel connected from the phone to a nearby cellular antenna and switch. The challenge with such devices is that they are produced in quantities of millions, they cannot be easily upgraded, and are under intense cost pressure. Consumer electronics experiences price pressure but much simpler to develop and maintain. Wireless telecommunications infrastructure, by way of contrast, faces much less cost pressure, is less complex overall compared to smartphone development, and finally is easily upgraded and maintained. An executive moving from an infrastructure manufacturer may have little experience in intensive cost management. In addition, an infrastructure executive likely never experienced the pressure of recalling thousands of products in the field that could not be upgraded. Finally, a consumer electronics executive moving to a developer and manufacturer of smartphones may never have had to grapple with a $100 million development budget for a product that required 2 years to develop. Bringing in a savior who apparently knows the business well may end up being an executive who knows little about the nuts and bolts of the business he or she is being asked to manage. This may be an obvious point when considering executives from clearly unrelated industries, but may also be a sleeping factor with outside executives who are an apparent good fit—but are not at all.

Companies in need of a turnaround may be attracted to executives who were successful in unrelated businesses. It is natural for a company to hear about the success and consequently may seek to recruit one such executive to reenergize the company with some new ideas. Unlike an executive who originates from an apparently similar, yet quite different operation, an executive from an unrelated business will bring not only fresh ideas to the company but high risk as well.

Pointers for how to fail:

1. Assume that the expertise of the outsider is a good fit.
2. Believe that the outsider understands the company.
3. Accept what the outsider tells you at face value during the recruiting process.
4. Be attracted to the unfamiliar.

Successful Growth and Change by M&A

It is difficult to grow a business. It requires effort, focus, attention to detail, knowledge of the industry and customers, and finally a deep intuitive understanding of how to attain and maintain a competitive advantage. Not every leader can lead a business to successful growth and profitability, even when they are brought in for this express purpose. There are no shortcuts to business success. However, there is an apparent shortcut to dramatically increasing the revenue of the business, and this is through the acquisition of another company. The idea is instead of organically growing the business and its revenues, creating a step-function increase in revenues overnight by acquiring a major competitor. Like many failed change management approaches, acquisition-based revenue growth is a shortcut to success. Because it can be exciting and tempting, this change strategy is often undertaken. Unfortunately, the results of "change by M&A" prove illusory.

One such example involves a telecommunications infrastructure manufacturer holding approximately 80 percent market share within a niche market. Sales had slowed from peak growth in this market thereby making the fight to hold on to and possibly grow the business more frenetic. Increasingly, customers in this market made the safe choice and used the dominant manufacturer for the reduced remaining infrastructure needs. The business conditions made it difficult for the manufacturer holding the second-place position in the market. As sales declined for the second-place manufacturer, the argument for research and development investment for the next generation of products grew weaker. The company elected to instead "throw in the towel" and reached out to the first-place competitor to begin negotiations to be acquired. This gesture was viewed as a fantastic opportunity to significantly grow the company and its revenues. Further, it sent the message to the telecommunications world that a tough competitor had been defeated. The prospect of a quick turnaround in an otherwise slowing market was celebrated by senior management. The celebration was premature (Figure 7.5).

Figure 7.5 Acquiring a competitor

As it often happens in acquisitions, the expected increased revenues in this acquisition failed to materialize. There are many reasons for why this happens, but most of these reasons materialized in the telecommunication acquisition example. To begin with, most of the clients of the number one supplier appreciated having a second vendor in place for competitive reasons. Two significant vendors were observed to "battle it out" in the marketplace when it came to price as well as innovation. When this was replaced with a near-monopoly situation, customers naturally became concerned and began to seek out current vendors playing on the periphery of the market to build them up to be worthy vendors competing for business. Some customers also began to consider forms of vertical integration by attempting to piece together infrastructure with off-the-shelf components and in-house software. The net result was a reduction from expected additional acquisition-related sales.

A second intended goal of acquisition is cost reduction. When two competitors become a single company, factories and research and development may be consolidated. There are complications, however, that naturally arise in such consolidation. The acquired competitor is likely to employ different technologies and architecture in their products making it essential to retain key knowledgeable personnel. Also, the consolidation of factories naturally requires retooling, and this takes time and effort. Finally, one way to reduce cost is to eliminate products that once competed head-to-head with the acquiring company. While this is desirable for cost reduction purposes, it may not be desirable for customers who hold a large installed base of products from the acquired company. The ongoing repair, maintenance, and upgrades required by the customers with an installed base of equipment also require that a level of development, manufacturing, and technical support capability be retained. The anticipated cost reduction is not achieved within a short-term time horizon. Instead, costs increases are incurred for plant consolidation, manufacturing transfer, retention of key people, and finally termination of employees along with the closure of competitor operations.

The attempt to change the company through an acquisition in this case failed. The market continued to decline, the expected increases in sales did not happen as planned, and cost increased rather than decreased. Further, the exit of a major competitor in the business was viewed by customers as well as the investment community as a signal of industry decline. This was reinforced by the competitor who sold the business to the market share leader. The proceeds of the sale and the key people who remained in the company were shifted to newer and more forward-looking technology. The market leader left with serving a declining market was saddled with additional work as well as cost and was forced to focus its energies on a market quickly becoming obsolete. The apparent loser in the market went on to bigger and better things, while the acquiring company slid into oblivion as the market collapsed.

Growth by acquisition is also targeted by companies who seek to grow by acquiring organizations that do not compete directly, yet if acquired, could add additional geographical coverage to the company. Telecommunications companies, after the divestiture of the Bell System in 1982, created several regional operators referred to as the "Baby Bells." Over the next 20 years as competing technologies evolved with the explosion of the Internet and wireless technologies, regional companies gradually began to merge with others as well as acquire other telecommunications service providers in other geographical areas. The addition of new coverage areas offered irresistible opportunities to grow revenue overnight and reduce costs where possible through consolidation. While such acquisitions did lead to additional revenue, the opportunity for cost reduction through consolidation proved more difficult than anticipated. The long history of the Bell Companies in the regions created insular cultures that were difficult to integrate. Each had unique processes and sought to influence the acquiring company by taking the lead on initiatives and processes that were implemented far outside of the original regional territory of the company. In the end, the attempt to change the company by acquiring what amounted to a step-function growth of revenue and territory enjoyed mixed results. The new company that resulted, instead of a larger company that was changed for the better, became a collection of "warring tribes."

Pointers for how to fail:

1. Acquire a major competitor during the final stages of market decline.
2. Assume that customer buying patterns will not change in the absence of multiple competitors in the marketplace.
3. Overlook the expense of maintaining and supporting acquired product lines.
4. Build a larger company with a collection of smaller companies that seek to lead rather than follow the lead of the acquirer.

CHAPTER 8

Execution Problems

Failure to Implement

We have long been criticized for having problems with quality. We will therefore implement six-sigma as part of our company turnaround.

The adoption of a quality process methodology is a noble undertaking and one that can pay dividends for companies who successfully implement it. However, process frameworks such as six-sigma, the "Baldridge" initiative, or others such as the CMM (Capability Maturity Model) are far from easy to implement. Further, executives who see in these frameworks a means for turning around a company often are unaware of the implications of adoption. Quality systems are by their nature process-focused. The idea behind them is that the control of the systems that produce products and services in an operation will result in quality outcomes. It is the process or processes that are controlled in a high-quality operation rather than the quality of each individual product itself. What executives fail to consider in the adoption of such quality management-driven change initiatives is that implementing a process-focused methodology requires process discipline. This means that employees, including executives, cannot simply do what they may want to do using ad hoc methods. Instead, they must respond to the issues of the day by means of following a defined process. The reason for the word "discipline" in the term "process-discipline" is that it is very difficult to follow processes when all instincts lead executives to take independent, ad hoc actions to address issues. Management by process constrains what executives can do. Executives are no longer kings but are actors in the organization who play a specific important role. They make hard decisions at important process milestones. They report status, good or bad, to clients, employees, and directors. They hire and fire as required. They point the way forward for the purposes of competitive advantage. However, such actions occur in the context of associated business processes. As soon as an executive understands the process constraints that limit executive power, the desire to support change via the implementation of a quality management framework begins to fade. The change goal announced with great fanfare therefore remains unimplemented, perhaps in a way analogous to what King John would have done had he become aware of what the Magna Carta would do to constrain future kingly action (Figure 8.1).

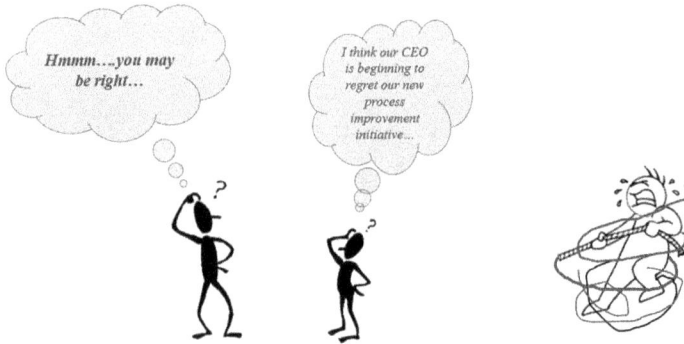

Figure 8.1 Process management and constraints

There are other circumstances where company executives fully support the proposed change, but the company fails to implement due to a lack of knowledge and capability. To make an analogy, consider that every football team desires to go to the Super Bowl, but only those teams with the capability to do so succeed. To illustrate this point, consider a company that is failing in the market due to its inability to launch products on time and within a regular annual cycle. Competitors in the industry would release at least two or more products per year in the spring and fall, but perhaps more when different products are launched in Europe, Asia, Africa, and the Americas. It was therefore dictated by the CEO of the parent company of the international telecommunications company that the company from now on would develop products on time and launch product multiple times per year just as competitors did. But, outside of the visible result of multiple product launches per year by competitors, what specifically did the competitors do that the company seeking change was not doing? Behind the scenes of the multiple product launches per year was a deep process infrastructure that organized development and portfolio decision-making spanning from the development of components to product platforms, and finished products. This process created the illusion of having the ability to develop and launch multiple products simultaneously. In reality, major competitors planned ahead in the 3- to 5-year range, determined what platforms would be needed to support multiple product iterations, and finally decided what components would be needed to support platform development. Although multiple products were launched across the globe twice per year, the same core platform was used along with customization and feature additions for each market. Doing this required a high degree of foresight, planning, and analysis of market and macroenvironment and demographic trends. Further, such processes required the discipline to commission the development of components today for products that may not materialize for another 5 years. Without such a process, an individual "from scratch" product development effort would take at least 18 to 24 months.

While delivering multiple products each year is a desirable change initiative, the implementation of such a goal requires both the understanding of what needs to be accomplished in order to achieve it and the process discipline to undertake it. The company seeking this goal failed to implement it because it lacked both the know-how and the accompanying process that happened. This can be observed by inspecting the product development process that was not able to support either timely product launch or the launch of multiple products. Instead of a structured planning and product line development process stretching out for three to 5 years, the company seeking change typically commissioned development projects in response to events, market shifts, or product launches from competitors. Events triggering the typical product development cycle that roughly follows this pattern:

1. External market trigger for new product.
2. Mad scramble on the part of the product planning department to create a highly desirable product specification without regard to the feasibility of development.

3. The design teams struggle to understand the technical and market requirements from the customer while at the same time arguing and negotiating with corporate product planning.

The product planning philosophy was to push the design teams as much as possible and accept nothing less than the ideal product based on comparison of competitor specifications and client requests. No thought was given regarding engineering capabilities, available platforms or components, or concerns regarding risk. This ad hoc trigger-driven process was to push even if it did not seem to make sense in hopes of inspiring some breakthrough. The ad hoc process continued as follows:

1. Frenetic activity ensued to identify possible technologies to create a workable product. This included chipsets, protocol stacks, software, firmware, and other components.
2. Time was wasted over a period of months negotiating with corporate executives and product planning managers, leaving approximately 1 year to develop what would typically take 2 to 3 years to develop from scratch.

This typical development cycle along with severe time constraints led to the development team adopting a very high-risk approach in order to get the product done in the required time frame. A more workable low-risk approach could not be considered because doing so would require that the company acknowledge that the schedule for delivery would be far behind what the company had committed to the market. Of course, the commitment was given to key customers by executives prior to conducting any feasibility study with the development team nor with any acknowledgment that no components nor platform technologies were in place.

The high-risk development strategy adopted by the company led over the years to several "runaway software development" projects. The software defects revealed in testing led to fixes that, once implemented, led to more defects. The defect resolution curve in such a runaway project failed to converge. Instead, in these situations, the defects continued to increase in spite of significant effort to correct them.

With multiple product delays and development failures, the engineers involved in development recognized that a more advanced management system would be required and therefore began to lobby senior management for change in how product development is managed if the goal of multiple products per year were ever to be achieved. It became clear to the development team that the mission to develop a next-generation product would require some stability in the product development process, some additional structure, and finally some forward-looking market projections to avoid last-minute reactions to market triggers without sufficient time to develop products. It was also clear that this approach to product development did not exist in the company. It was decided that the satellite operations of the corporate parent with the highest level of process expertise would focus not only on product development, but on driving process improvement throughout the company so that the maturity level of the parent company could be improved. Some explicit strategic goals were as follows:

1. Adopt a structured product development process locally and continually promote it within the parent company.
2. Shift from a functional organization to a true matrix organization so that multiple projects could be pursued at the same time.
3. Shift to the incremental software development method (and away from the existing waterfall method practiced throughout the company).
4. Adopt a product line methodology to focus the organization on building components and platforms in advance of products in an effort to better respond to market requirements for frequent product refreshes (and avoid the mad scramble to integrate products on the fly from technologies available from various vendors at any given time).
5. Implement a process improvement infrastructure within the local company to craft improvements, document them, and promote the processes as well as the process improvement methodology to the parent company.

The first step in pursuing improvements in the product development process was to attempt to clarify the roles and responsibilities of product development being carried out throughout the world. The existing model of product development assigned a development team to each market. Very little was shared between market teams making the corresponding maturity of documentation and design processes limited. The local teams could react (and often did) to ad hoc direction with a minimum of coordination between teams. While this method of resource allocation supported optimal flexibility, it also led to high costs. Success in a given product development team occurred when the team was fortunate enough to have a strong project manager to drive the project over the finish line. Should the team find themselves behind schedule or over budget, limited support could be obtained from other teams or corporate offices due to the semi-autonomous structure of the globally distributed organizations and resulting lack of standardization (Figure 8.2).

Market Responsibility Method
Each design center is responsible for developing products for their own market

	Corporate Reference Design (Platform)	Product Line Method	Market Responsibility Method	Hybrid Method
Cost	LOW	MEDIUM	HIGH	MEDIUM
Design Sophistication	HIGH	MEDIUM	LOW	MEDIUM
Architecture Skill	HIGH	MEDIUM	LOW	MEDIUM
Management Sophistication	HIGH	MEDIUM	LOW	MEDIUM
	Corporate Reference Design	Product Line Method	**Market Responsibility Method**	Hybrid Method
Common Design Process	Required	Required	Not Required	Required
Common Documentation & Systems	Required	Required	Not Required	Required
Strong, Clear Development Strategy	Required	Required	Not Required	Required
Strong Up-Front Planning Systems	Required	Required	Preferred	Required
Strong Project Management	Required	Required	Preferred	Preferred

Figure 8.2 Market responsibility method

Leadership from the development groups sought an improved solution to the organization of teams around specific global markets. One popular approach that had been employed by global companies was to create a platform referred to as a reference design at the corporate headquarters, and then have design centers in local markets customize a product based on the corporate reference design and do so in a structured and modular way. This approach was considered far more efficient than organizing according to a loose confederation of semi-autonomous operations supporting markets around the world. However, it also required a high degree of complex system development and standardization skills to create and manage such a design operation. It also required a long-term market focus and strong process discipline with contributing management skills such as project management and documentation creation and management. The products historically produced by corporate R&D were weak in terms of architecture and not suitable for the extraction of a global reference design. Regardless of the attractiveness of this approach, the corporate product development headquarters acknowledged that this strategy was not feasible (Figure 8.3).

Detailed hardware and software reference design ("platform") is completed by corporate office.
Design must be highly modular (plug and play type) to minimize local modification effort.
Strong documentation, strong design control, and strong formal management systems, common process & procedures.
Small local teams modify product. Work is minimized because corporate design is very clean, modular, and well documented.

	Design (Platform)	Method	Method	
Cost	LOW	MEDIUM	HIGH	MEDIUM
Design Sophistication	HIGH	MEDIUM	LOW	MEDIUM
Architecture Skill	HIGH	MEDIUM	LOW	MEDIUM
Management Sophistication	HIGH	MEDIUM	LOW	MEDIUM

	Corporate Reference Design	Product Line Method	Market Responsibility Method	Hybrid Method
Common Design Process	Required	Required	Not Required	Required
Common Documentation & Systems	Required	Required	Not Required	Required
Strong, Clear Development Strategy	Required	Required	Not Required	Required
Strong Up-Front Planning Systems	Required	Required	Preferred	Required
Strong Project Management	Required	Required	Preferred	Preferred

Figure 8.3 Corporate reference design method

An alternative to the corporate reference design was to assign product line responsibilities to each product development operation regardless of location. Given the global convergence toward common standards such as GSM and 3G, the emphasis on assigning development teams to support specific markets began to seem misplaced. It was expected that some efficiency could be gained by allowing each operation to focus on their respective strengths. Further, it allowed for continued semi-autonomous operation that did not require the process discipline associated with multisite development collaboration on each product. The downside to this form of reorganizing is that multiple development teams separated by geography would need to support product launches in multiple factories and countries around the world (Figure 8.4).

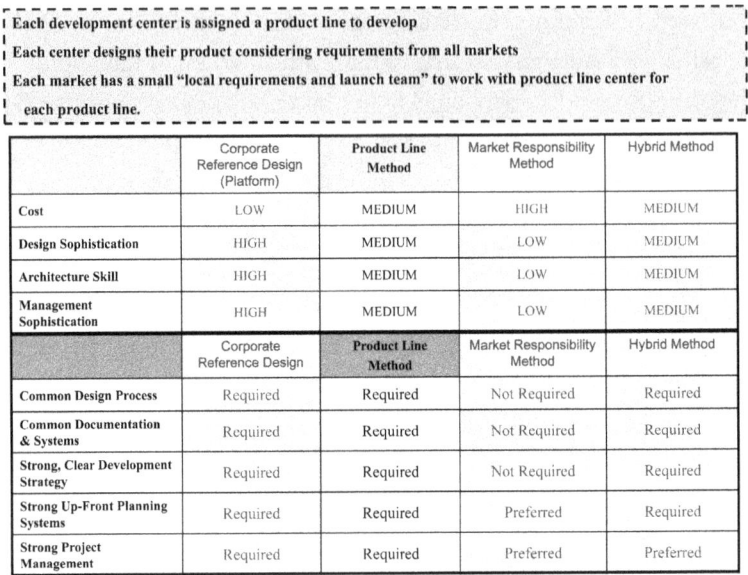

| Each development center is assigned a product line to develop |
| Each center designs their product considering requirements from all markets |
| Each market has a small "local requirements and launch team" to work with product line center for each product line. |

	Corporate Reference Design (Platform)	Product Line Method	Market Responsibility Method	Hybrid Method
Cost	LOW	MEDIUM	HIGH	MEDIUM
Design Sophistication	HIGH	MEDIUM	LOW	MEDIUM
Architecture Skill	HIGH	MEDIUM	LOW	MEDIUM
Management Sophistication	HIGH	MEDIUM	LOW	MEDIUM
	Corporate Reference Design	Product Line Method	Market Responsibility Method	Hybrid Method
Common Design Process	Required	Required	Not Required	Required
Common Documentation & Systems	Required	Required	Not Required	Required
Strong, Clear Development Strategy	Required	Required	Not Required	Required
Strong Up-Front Planning Systems	Required	Required	Preferred	Required
Strong Project Management	Required	Required	Preferred	Preferred

Figure 8.4 Product line method

Finally, a mix of various approaches to organizing global product development was considered. The benefit of this approach was that it added a layer of discipline onto globally distributed product development centers while also allowing for some ad hoc product and technology assignments. Ultimately, a hybrid method appeared to be like the structure already in place. In fact, it was observed that although the current structure was said to be one of "market responsibility," in practice, each local product development organization tended to be assigned to activities by corporate engineering that suited them based on the market or industry trigger du jour (Figure 8.5).

| Some mixing of each method. |
| For example, local teams can have some market responsibility, but they use some |
| existing design, or reference design to simplify work. |

	Corporate Reference Design (Platform)	Product Line Method	Market Responsibility Method	**Hybrid Method**
Cost	LOW	MEDIUM	HIGH	MEDIUM
Design Sophistication	HIGH	MEDIUM	LOW	MEDIUM
Architecture Skill	HIGH	MEDIUM	LOW	MEDIUM
Management Sophistication	HIGH	MEDIUM	LOW	MEDIUM
	Corporate Reference Design	Product Line Method	Market Responsibility Method	**Hybrid Method**
Common Design Process	Required	Required	Not Required	Required
Common Documentation & Systems	Required	Required	Not Required	Required
Strong, Clear Development Strategy	Required	Required	Not Required	Required
Strong Up-Front Planning Systems	Required	Required	Preferred	Required
Strong Project Management	Required	Required	Preferred	Preferred

Figure 8.5 Hybrid method

After ongoing discussion, comparison, and conflict among the global product development stakeholders, the decision was announced to restructure global product development using the product line method. It was hoped that the new structure would better focus the efforts of each team so that the company was better positioned to produce multiple products per year (Figure 8.6).

	Corporate Reference Design (Platform)	Product Line Method	Market Responsibility Method	Hybrid Method
Cost	LOW	MEDIUM	HIGH	MEDIUM
Design Sophistication	HIGH	MEDIUM	LOW	MEDIUM
Architecture Skill	HIGH	MEDIUM	LOW	MEDIUM
Management Sophistication	HIGH	MEDIUM	LOW	MEDIUM
	Corporate Reference Design	Product Line Method	Market Responsibility Method	Hybrid Method
Common Design Process	Required	Required	Not Required	Required
Common Documentation & Systems	Required	Required	Not Required	Required
Strong, Clear Development Strategy	Required	Required	Not Required	Required
Strong Up-Front Planning Systems	Required	Required	Preferred	Required
Strong Project Management	Required	Required	Preferred	Preferred

Figure 8.6 System comparison

Structure versus Governance

While restructuring held the promise of improved performance, restructuring was but one component of the overall improvement effort. The new structure required management oversight or governance in order to foster decision-making, ensure collaboration where necessary, to distribute and manage product development budgets, and finally to ensure the alignment of all product development operations with the corporate product and business strategy. In fact, it could be said that above all, governance, rather than organizational structure, was the real problem to be solved. Although global product development efforts involved costs ranging from the tens to hundreds of millions, work assignments as well as budgets were determined informally by a single corporate engineering manager in the breakroom in company headquarters. The informal approach proved problematic, particularly since assignments and budgets tended to change frequently (Figure 8.7).

To make the most out of the newly implemented global product development structure, the globally distributed product development operations lobbied for a more structured approach to decision-making. The launch of multiple products per year by each team was unfeasible when budgets and product roadmaps changed on a regular basis. To attempt to minimize ad hoc decision-making, it was proposed to formalize the decision-making process by moving the decision-making from a single informal point of failure to a team of sponsoring executives. The idea was floated of creating an entity called the "product development board." It was accepted by the corporate executives primarily because it supported greater visibility of budget decisions by the general manager of the division. Further, the product development board provided a formal means for sales and marketing executives to have more involvement in the commissioning of product development projects (Figure 8.8).

The revised organizational structure paired with a strengthened decision-making structure provided some stability to the management of product development. However, the traditional ad hoc decision-making culture continued to get in the way of the process-oriented focus that would support the launch of multiple projects per year. It was recognized that a more comprehensive restructuring of product development

Current Situation: Informal ad-hoc meetings govern global product development

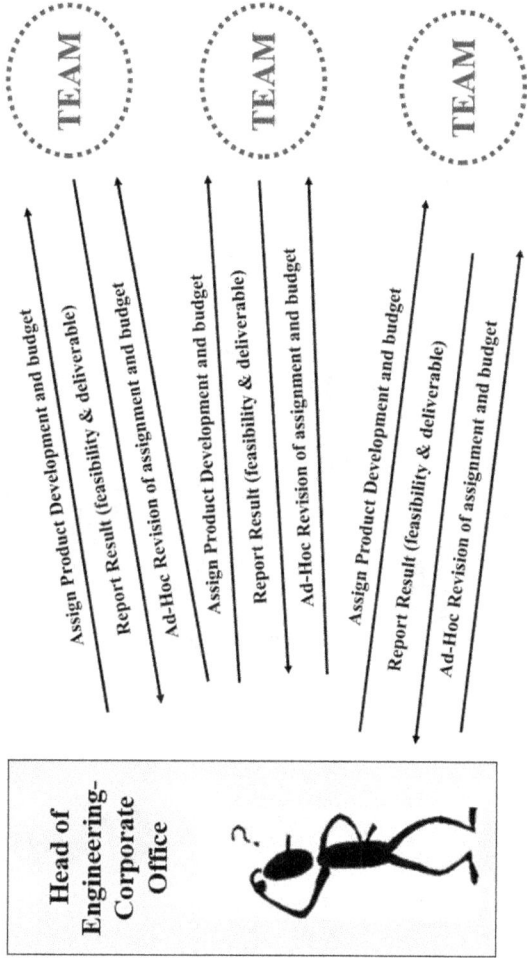

Head of Engineering-Corporate Office

Assign Product Development and budget
Report Result (feasibility & deliverable)
Ad-Hoc Revision of assignment and budget

Assign Product Development and budget
Report Result (feasibility & deliverable)
Ad-Hoc Revision of assignment and budget

Assign Product Development and budget
Report Result (feasibility & deliverable)
Ad-Hoc Revision of assignment and budget

TEAM

TEAM

TEAM

Figure 8.7 Ad hoc global product development

Initial Idea: Shift from Individual to Executive Group Decision-Making

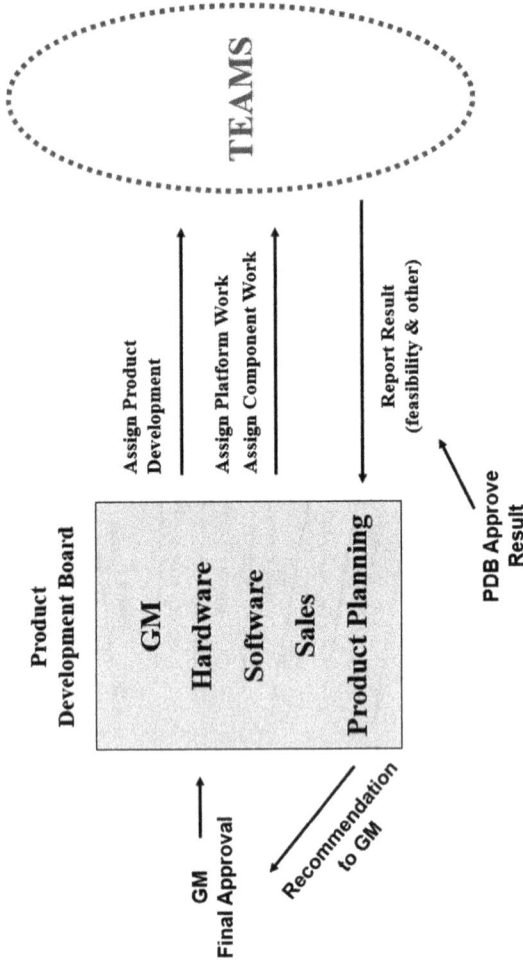

Product Development Board

GM
Hardware
Software
Sales
Product Planning

Assign Product Development

Assign Platform Work
Assign Component Work

Report Result (feasibility & other)

PDB Approve Result

GM Final Approval

Recommendation to GM

TEAMS

Figure 8.8 From individual to group decision-making

governance was needed. The first step in realizing this vision was the attempt at the implementation of the Product and Cycle-time Excellence (PACE) as pioneered by the consulting firm PRTM (and now championed by the Product Development Management Association [PDMA]). This process was first implemented in local product development operations and then promoted and lobbied for in the corporate engineering office. The problem with this effort to influence the corporate office to adopt new process is in the recognition that a problem exists with the current systems and processes. An early effort was made to promote the PACE model to corporate executives by presenting a copy of the book *Setting the PACE in Product Development* by Michael McGrath of the product development consulting firm PRTM (Pittiglio, Rabin, Todd & McGrath). Representatives of local product development teams followed up a few months later in a trip to corporate headquarters when an engineering executive was asked "What do you think about the book we gave you to read?" The response was "Oh-yeah, we are already doing it" (Figure 8.9).

The next effort to establish the product-line methodology was to attempt to implement the processes locally, produce results, and then use the outcomes to promote the processes globally.

These efforts were a beginning, but culture change was a constant battle. Eventually, the corporate executives saw the need for an improved development process and IBM was brought in to lead the effort. Principles from process improvement activities in the local company were incorporated in the PACE and product-line organization effort. However, it was observed that the parent company carried out the same practices in product development that were always done. The only real change was the incorporation of existing practices within new templates and nomenclature provided by IBM. Elaborate product line and component development roadmaps were created to support the vision of launching multiple products per year, but were never explicitly executed. The focus on individual products alone drove all activities in the company. This led to the local development team adopting a strategy to develop a product in such a way that a platform could be extracted from it on completion. Included in this effort was the partnership between the local development organization with industry partners who could supply highly structured hardware and

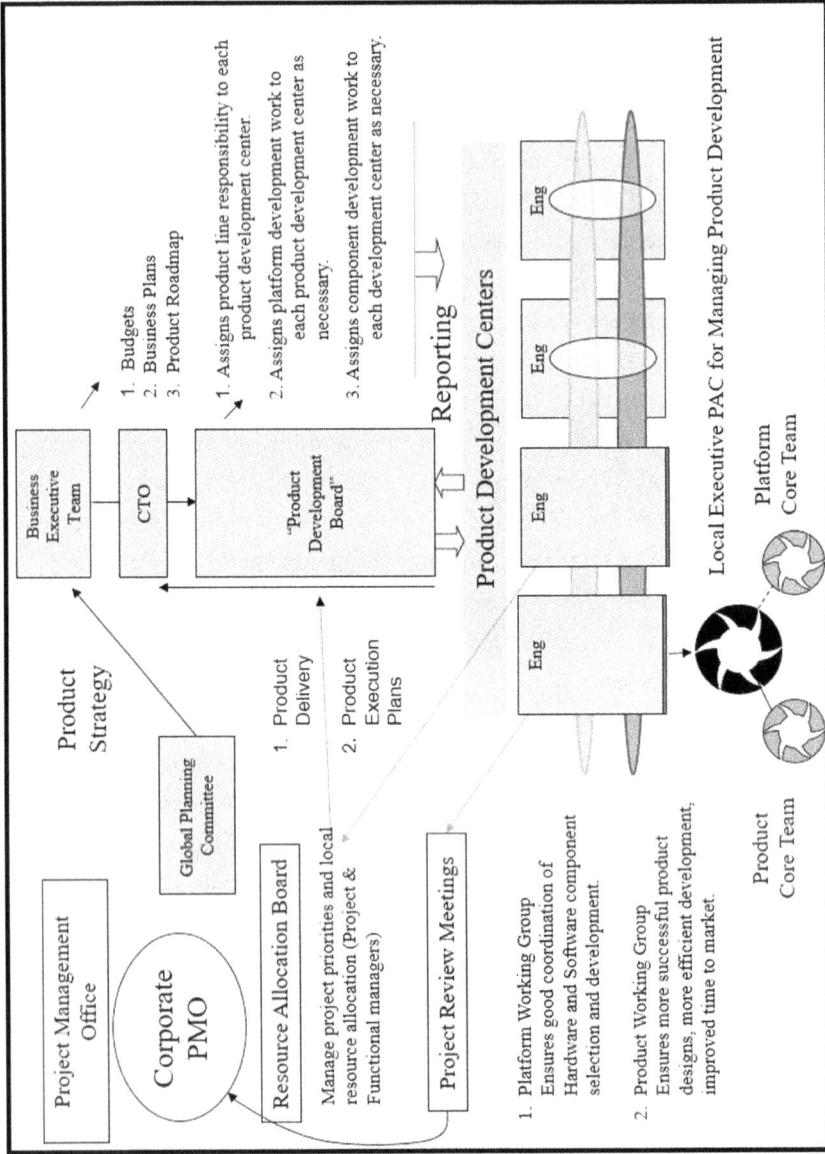

Figure 8.9 Global decision-making structure

software components to support platform and product-line architecture. The structured software in this platform and the lack of know-how on the part of corporate engineering to understand it or modify it provided hope that a strong platform could be built locally and eventually adopted globally. There was some discussion by corporate engineering about attempting to port software features from products in which the company was known to be strong, such as audio, video, and other consumer electronics products. However, the corporate code base was so corrupt and so tightly coupled to individual products that gleaning functionality from audiovisual products and porting to the new platform was proved to be impossible. As an example of corrupted code and weak architecture, it was not uncommon to find extensive use of global variables throughout unstructured, poorly documented, and non-object-oriented code.

The goal of launching multiple products per year proved to be elusive. The goal was announced and endlessly promoted, and many supporting moves and restructuring were carried out to support it. In the end, the company was not capable of implementing the grand strategy that the company set out to achieve and failed as a result.

Pointers for how to fail:

1. Commit to change without understanding the implications.
2. Promote change that requires managers to do what they are never going to do.
3. Embark on change that ignores the culture, history, and fundamental capability of the company.
4. Attempt change on a grand scale with managers having only small-scale experience.

PART III

Lessons for Change Managers

There are two main principles that lead to successful change management. The first is to do the right thing, and the second is to avoid doing the wrong thing. Part II identified many examples of actions taken in the course of change management initiatives that are almost certain to lead to failure. To be successful in light of these mistakes is to avoid repeating history and to not take these actions. In Part III positive steps are identified that, if followed, increase the chances that outcomes sought in change initiatives will be met. This examination of positive action begins with the concerted effort to definitively understand the underlying issues so that the change initiative is more likely to solve the right problem.

Chapter 9

The Road to Success

Causality and Root Cause Analysis

It has been observed that solving the wrong problem is a common ailment in change management. What then should managers do so that the chances of identifying the right problem is improved? There is an effective method that middle managers and individual contributors often use, yet executives managing change initiatives seem to forget. Root cause analysis using the "Five Whys" approach helps executives go beyond "scratching the surface" and prevent the usual knee-jerk reaction of jumping on an easy surface solution. The five whys process is often accompanied by the use of the fishbone diagram where underlying causes visually branch from intermediate steps in the analysis of ultimate causation. The key is "causation" and ensuring that observed linkages between events and outcomes are correctly assumed. Management brings with it the tendency to employ error in judgment when thinking through cause and effect. For example, a common error involves "post hoc ergo propter hoc"—Latin for "after this, therefore because of this." In management, this error occurs by noticing that "event A" occurs followed by "outcome B," followed by assuming that A caused B. As an example, a company is failing, a new CEO is hired, and results improve. It is easy to assume that "A caused B," but making this connection requires a deep dive into the evidence. Ultimately, root cause analysis is a form of diagnosis. In the same way that a medical doctor seeks to understand the reason for illness, a change manager seeks to understand underlying organizational diseases correctly. Without this understanding, a change agent is rather like a doctor prescribing the wrong medicine because of the failure to correctly diagnose the disease.

Learning the Forgotten Art of Diagnosis

A change management initiative has a clear beginning and ending, and it is complex, unique, and employs resources in order to achieve the desired goals. A change management initiative may therefore be defined as a project because the characteristics of change initiatives align well with the definition of a project. A project formally begins with a project charter, and the project charter includes a brief statement of scope. Scope is linked to the project requirements, and requirements are that which the deliverables of the project are intended to satisfy. A change manager therefore acts as a project manager whose first job is to understand the requirements of the project and develop the project scope. In essence, the project manager begins with WHAT needs to change. However, as is in the case of developing requirements, organizational problems are complex. Determining what needs to change is therefore a nontrivial matter. Change management requirements involve the analysis of a complex system; so keeping Senge's ideas in mind regarding the underlying complexity of organizations, requirements and scope of the change initiative are more reliably developed by collecting multiple sources of evidence in order to define the problem. It bears remembering that it is not uncommon for executives to hear multiple reasons daily for why something is not working. However, this is anecdotal evidence and cannot be accepted at face value (Figure 9.1).

> Rule One: Anecdotal Evidence is not enough!

Figure 9.1 Anecdotal evidence is not enough

What Needs to Change? How Can You Know?

Achieving a holistic understanding of the root cause or the underlying problem in which a change initiative is intended to solve requires analysis and research. The question for the change agent or company leadership then becomes, "What kind of research is necessary, and how is it done?" There are two broad-based approaches to research, and these are quantitative and qualitative research techniques. It is tempting for the leadership to focus first on quantitative research techniques given that quantitative research is, by its association with numbers, considered as hard science. On the other hand, quantitative research typically relies on survey instruments for data collection. Survey instruments are a quick and efficient means for collecting data, but what results is only a snapshot of individual perceptions. Quantitative research therefore "learns a very little from a lot"—a snapshot from a small sample—which is used to test theory and hypotheses. When attempting to better understand the phenomena, while qualitative research techniques provide significant depth of analysis, it does not mean that numeric data cannot be employed in the research of the phenomena. Sales trends, financial trends, transaction data—all of this information is useful to aid in drawing conclusions regarding the root cause. The numeric data combined with qualitative data such as interviews aid in building up a complete picture of "what is going on." This is a different approach from the typical practice of quantitative research that tests hypotheses (Figure 9.2).

Understanding what needs to change requires a depth of analysis and consideration. A good way to achieve such depth is to approach the diagnosis of the organization through qualitative research techniques. Qualitative research uses an inductive approach that is used to develop theory. In other words, the theory regarding the nature of the problem(s) faced by the organization emerges from a close, often iterative, analysis of evidence in various forms collected from the organization. In some ways, this approach is akin to root cause analysis and the "five whys." The root cause of any organization-wide problem is well considered and goes beneath a surface consideration of the issues. Still, the solution that results is only a theory regarding the underlying cause of the problem. Therefore, when a leader of an organization begins a change management initiative, the individual is doing so based on a

> But why not quantitative techniques? Isn't that "hard science"?

Quantitative

1. Typically relies on survey instruments
2. Takes a snapshot of individual perceptions
3. Quick and efficient
4. "Learn a little about a lot"
5. Used to test theory and hypotheses

Qualitative

1. Typically relies on documentary analysis, interviews, focus groups, observations
2. In-depth capture of individual and group perceptions
3. Labor intensive
4. "Learn a lot about a little"
5. Used to build theory

Diagnosis: Developing a theory for what needs to change.

Figure 9.2 Qualitative versus quantitative methods

theory of what is wrong with the organization. A change in initiative is therefore akin to a test of a hypothesis. Hypothesis testing is usually associated with quantitative research. Data are collected and evaluated statistically, and the hypothesis is accepted or rejected. Qualitative inductive analysis and quantitative hypothesis testing therefore go "hand in hand." Theory is built or, in this case, a theory of the underlying root cause of the problem is developed, and then tested once developed. It is therefore reasonable that the diagnosis—or theory regarding the underlying problems in the organization—is developed using inductive, qualitative research techniques. Qualitative research relies on documentary analysis, interviews, focus groups, and observations. It is an in-depth capture of individual and group perceptions and is therefore more labor-intensive. Unlike quantitative techniques, qualitative research "learns a great deal from a little" or narrow context. This is what the manager, leader, or change agent needs for a complete and holistic diagnosis of the organization—an in depth understanding of what is wrong in the organization and what change is likely to be able to correct it. It is recommended therefore that diagnosis in change management employs qualitative research techniques in order to develop a theory regarding what in the organization needs to change.

Triangulation

In the same way that anecdotal evidence should not be accepted, no single source of evidence is capable of capturing the essence of the problems triggering the need for change. Multiple sources of evidence are required to arrive at a diagnosis of the underlying issue or problem. The idea is to analyze each source of evidence, compare them, contrast them, search for relationships and overall patterns, and finally synthesize conclusions. The term "triangulation" is used to describe this form of analysis, and as the name infers, at least three evidence sources should be brought to bear in the analysis. Such triangulation is often carried out within a court of law. A prosecuting attorney presents witness testimony and fingerprint evidence, and bank account records paint a picture of the apparent guilt of the defendant in order to achieve a conviction. Likewise, the change manager uses multiple evidence sources to gain a sense of what is really going on in the organization (Figure 9.3).

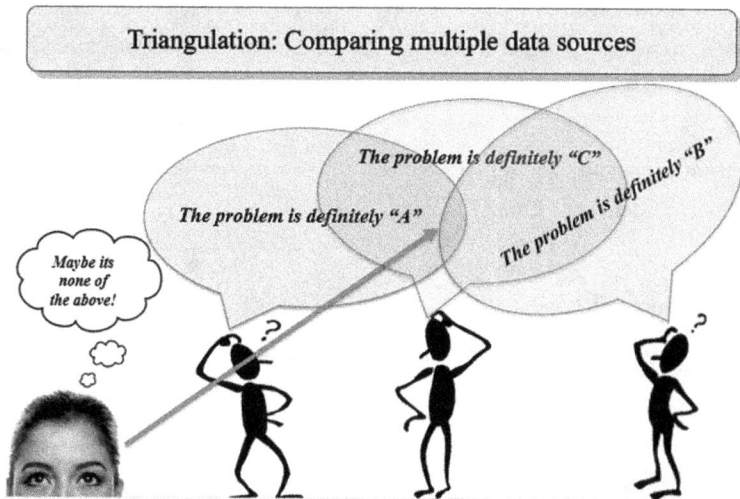

Figure 9.3 Triangulation of evidence sources

The Diagnosis Methodology

The Process: Phase 1

In order to be successful, a business must be grounded and confront the facts of the matter. The facts may well differ from what employees think they are (and say that they are), rather than what they are. For this reason, it is recommended that the process of diagnosis begins with collecting and analyzing internal documents. Internal documents ground the research by providing a factual record that forms the starting point for the following data collection efforts. Internal documents include e-mails, presentations, reports, process flows, and spreadsheets, which when analyzed and compared provide a clear picture of the issues faced by the organization. A few forms of qualitative data analysis may be undertaken with documentary evidence. For example, the documents may be ordered so that a historical timeline of events may be observed. Additionally, processes described in documents may be captured using flowcharting or swim-lane notation so that what function took an action or made a decision may be determined as well as how such action may have crossed organizational boundaries. Data-intensive documents such as spreadsheets and presentations may be summarized to capture performance information, patterns and trends, and disconnects between progress and plans. Finally, verbal information found in written reports, e-mails, and other documents may be thematically analyzed using qualitative data analysis techniques. This involves highlighting and coding important passages, combining multiple related passages to visualize themes, and by arranging the identified themes so that an overall picture or conceptual framework of the problem or issue under study emerges (Figure 9.4).

The Process: Phase 2

Once the initial documentary analysis is complete, it is recommended that the interim findings are prepared, presented, and discussed with a focus group for validation purposes. It is recommended that the members of the focus group should consist of a cross-section of 7 to 10 key people from the organization. The primary purpose of the focus group is that of validation. For example, the focus group session seeks to understand if the group agrees or disagrees with the interim findings. Also, it is determined whether the focus group has anything to add to the documentary analysis. Finally, the focus group session is recorded and transcribed, and qualitative data analysis is performed on the transcript of the recording. The results of the thematic analysis of the focus group transcript is used to refine and enhance the findings of the Phase 1 documentary analysis (Figure 9.5).

How do you perform analysis?

- Analyze text (such as interview transcripts)
- Identify and code key passages
- Collect and organize coded passages to form themes
- Organize themes to form a conceptual framework

Analogy:
Codes=Bricks
Organized codes (Theme) = Wall
Conceptual framework = Brick House

Figure 9.4 Performing analysis

Present findings to organizational focus group for validation

Use visuals! (Diagrams, flowcharts)

Helping the group visualize findings is key for participation and validation!

Figure 9.5 The focus group as means for validation

The Process: Phase 3

The validated summary of the two phases of data collection may now be used as the basis for discussion in one-on-one interviews with individuals selected from within the organization. A reasonable number of interviews would involve 15 to 20 employees drawn from different functional groups or departments. The number of people to be interviewed depends on a concept referred to as "saturation." Once interviews have proceeded to the point that no further new information is gleaned, the interview data collection may be terminated and the focus is shifted to the qualitative data analysis of the interviews (Figure 9.6).

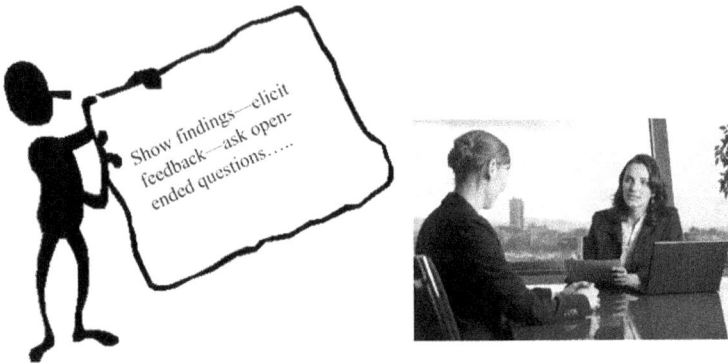

Figure 9.6 Use validated summary in one-on-one interviews

The individuals selected should not be drawn from those who participated in the focus group validation or provided documents for analysis. The selection of a different set of individuals for the interviewing phase allows for the diversity of viewpoints essential for triangulation. The multiple sources of evidence that are collected and analyzed therefore allows for a more comprehensive picture of the problem or issue under consideration, and further provides insights into possible solutions. As in the case of the focus group, each interview should be recorded and transcripts created for analysis (Figure 9.7).

Once again, the thematic analysis of the interviews is used to validate interim findings, and to supplement and finalize the conceptual framework and resulting theory or diagnosis regarding the exact nature of the problem to be addressed by a change management initiative.

The Process: Phase 4

In the final phase of the diagnosis research process, all previous participants are gathered for a review of the findings from the previous

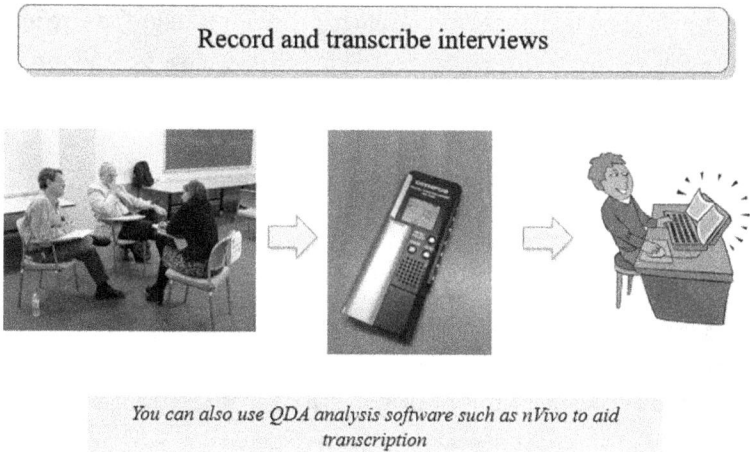

Figure 9.7 *Record and transcribe interviews*

three phases. This is a final validation step in the research and is used to both correct and, if necessary, confirm findings, and to aid in developing a final summary for presentation to the overall organization as well (Figure 9.8).

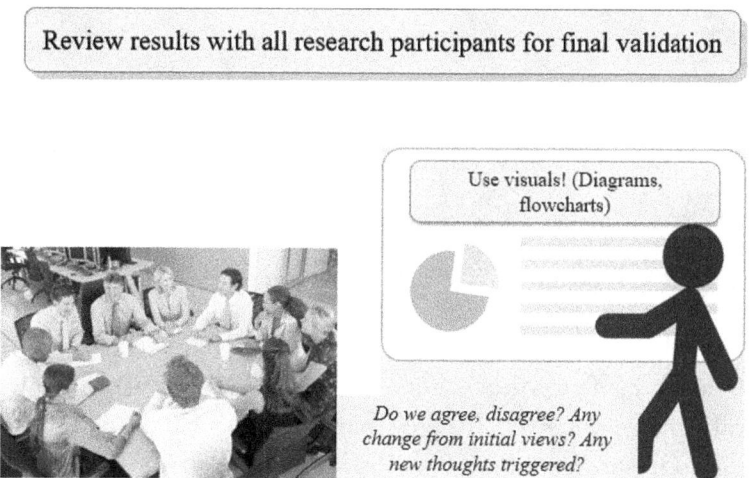

Figure 9.8 *Review results with all participants*

The final validation session is also used to develop a messaging strategy and brainstorm implementation plan approaches. It should be noted that the overall data collection process takes time and careful planning as well as effort. This alone is likely to prevent the snap judgment that tends to happen in the context of change decision-making. The diagnosis process helps ensure that executives seeking change move beyond surface consideration of issues.

Presenting the Diagnosis

It has been observed that formal change management frameworks focus on events referred to as "unfreezing," "defining the problem," and "creating a sense of urgency." The presentation of the diagnosis to the organization at large provides an opportunity for the leader of the change initiative to accomplish this by demonstrating that the change diagnosis resulted from an in-depth analysis process (Figure 9.9).

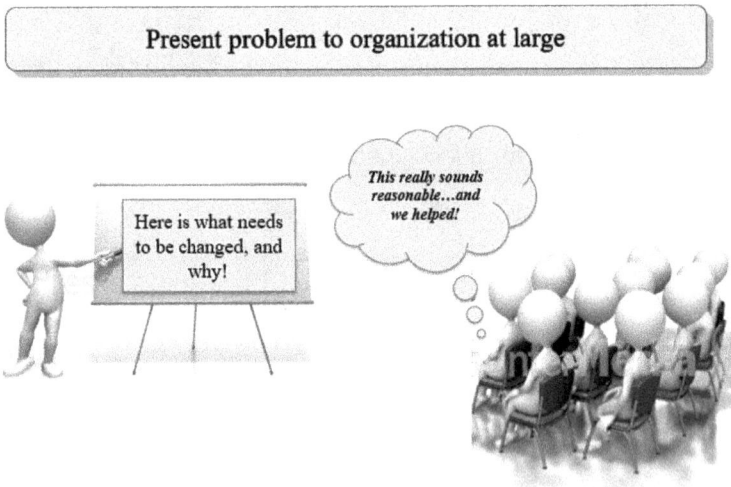

Figure 9.9 Presenting to the entire organization

Further, the diagnosis is observed to be derived not from the whim of the leader, but from a deep consideration of a broad range of stakeholders within the organization. The presentation therefore has the potential to gain acceptance and buy-in from the organization prior to carrying out the actual change initiative.

Diagnosis Is a Process

It is observed that diagnosis is an iterative process of collecting, analyzing, summarizing, and validating evidence collected from the organization.

The problem identified from this iterative approach becomes the starting point for the change initiative. The change initiative implements changes to strategy and processes designed to solve the problem identified in the diagnosis process. As a result, the change initiative is the test of the quality of the problem-solving process. Change does not end here. Data from the change initiative are collected and reviewed, and an unsuccessful result can trigger successive diagnosis cycles (Figure 9.10).

The Diagnosis Methodology

1. Collect and analyze documents
2. Summarize documentary analysis and prepare findings
3. Present findings to organizational focus group for validation
4. Use validated summary for as the basis for discussion in one-on-one interviews
   - Cross-section of organization: 15 to 20 people
5. Record and transcribe interviews
6. Perform QDA on interview transcripts to determine themes and overall picture of the problem(s)/issue(s) *[Conceptual framework]*
7. Review results with all research participants for final validation
8. Present problem to organization at large.

Figure 9.10 Summary of diagnosis methodology

What's Next?

It is at this point in the analysis that the change management models come into clearer focus. The bias toward implementation of change fits well with a change initiative that has resulted from an in-depth and well-researched diagnosis process. Such a process if followed will aid in preventing knee-jerk reactions from executives responding to internal or external triggers, jumping to conclusions, or the adoption of pet ideas.

Culture

A Japanese manager was once asked by a Western employee,

> Why is it that Japanese titles in the workplace seem so vague to Westerners? Also, why is it that Japanese job descriptions tend to be very general with overlapping roles—particularly from the point of view of Western employees?

The Japanese manager responded,

> Ah…that's easy. When a Japanese employee experiences great
> success—we want to share that success with all others within the
> group. Likewise, if a Japanese employee experiences failure, we do
> not want the employee to bear the blame all alone. We prefer to
> share!

This example provides insights into culture. A response such as this from
a Western manager would likely be very difficult to accept by employees—
a culture that celebrates individual achievement and rewards. While culture
is often viewed as an intangible factor, it is nonetheless very real in the
context of change. Each company tends to do things in a certain way, and
it is this "way" that can either incorporate the change effort into the insti-
tutional genetic map or reject it as a form or disease or invading ideology.
An examination of team development theory from the discipline of project
management provides some clues on how this works. According to Tuckman
(1977), teams progress through stages of development as they grow and
become effective. The process begins when teams come together and encounter each other as a working unit for the first time. This stage is called
forming and it includes the formalities of getting to know one another and
grasping the mission in which the team is assigned. Once the effort begins,
team members tend to engage in conflict as they sort out roles, responsibilities, and reporting hierarchy. This stage is referred to as *storming* because of
the conflict and the often-messy process involved in coming together as a
team. It is a storm of activity and it takes time to work through—often with
great difficulty. After the dust settles, the team begins to establish rules and
policies for working together. The rules of the team may not be explicitly
stated but represent the common understanding of how team members get
things done together. This stage is referred to as *norming* and it is norms
that appear to most impacted by change proposals pursued from outside
the team. The final stage in team development is *performing* and this is
a property that emerges once the team has grown to work together and
established implicit or explicit policies, norms, and working relationships.
In what ways does team development theory relate to change at the organizational level? Large organizations were once small organizations and, in
the same manner as project teams, they evolved over time and established

norms. Further, much of the work that gets done in large organizations today, be it product development work, R&D, or strategic initiatives, involves many teams (Figure 9.11).

One reason for viewing organizational change through the lens of team development is that team development theory illustrates the difficulty experienced by individuals in establishing working relationships and norms. Further, once this occurs and teams are performing effectively, they tend to be tightly bound together and resistant to outside influence and interference. Finally, the organization that an executive seeks to change may be composed almost exclusively of highly focused teams that are already on a path that they deem to be effective already. Proposing something different is likely to scramble existing teams or leave existing teams in place but with a different mission. Each of these impacts are likely to reset the phases of team development thereby forcing a large portion of the organization to return to the storming mode of operation. The noise created by this situation could well be a factor in the resistance associated with change proposals. Understanding culture is therefore rather like understanding a forest. Viewing culture from the team level and the micro-impact that change has on teams is like understanding the forest at the tree level. Without trees living in harmony there is no forest, so it is incumbent upon change managers to recognize change impact at the team level in light of team development theory.

Company culture also reveals itself in the language and terminology it uses, the values in which it places its emphasis, and the goals that are implicitly understood to be a good fit for the firm. A change of direction that is outside of accepted norms is likely to be viewed as a threat to the health of the firm. In some instances, the forces of resistance may think of their battle as one of good versus evil and will fight to the last breath to prevent the change. Effective change managers understand this and gradually socialize change ideas with the known resistance to help them see benefits as well as the rationale behind the change. It is always preferred to have the resistance "army" supporting and fighting for the change proposal rather than seeking to rally other employees to fight it at every step. For managers new to change, consider that change proposals are likely to impinge on the existing culture, and for better or worse, this will trigger a reaction. Change managers are well-advised to think ahead, study the culture, and understand it prior to seeking to change it.

Figure 9.11 Change and storming

Clarity, Practicality, and Tangibility

Much has been said about the lack of *clarity* in direction, for example, SMART versus DUMB goals. Having the right kind of goals in change management is no doubt essential for success. On the other hand, clarity goes beyond goal setting. Consider as an example a manager who seeks to change the company by adopting some new technology. The first question that comes to the minds of employees is likely to be "why?" Successful change managers will take steps to make it clear—be it a new product, market, process, technology, or customer. Some managers can make change clear at one level, but cannot get to the level needed for full comprehension and buy-in from the organization. Consider the following sequence of questions:

"We are going to acquire a company with a new technology that we will incorporate into all products!"

Question: Why?

"Because we will sell more product!"

Question: How do we know?

"Because customers love new technology!"

Question: If we sell more, will we be more profitable?

"The new technology will enable us to be more efficient and this will lead us to greater profitability!"

Question: How does the new technology make us more efficient?
Question: Do we know how to make products with this technology?
Question: Will we need additional factories?
Question: Will all of us require retraining on the new technology?
Question: Will there be layoffs because we are more efficient and require fewer workers?

Notice how the questions continue, but not the answers. The answers are not likely to be forthcoming—but when they are—they are often unconvincing. Clarity in change management means being able to break down the change in detail and fluently discuss its impact.

The *practicality* of the proposed change—or rather the lack of it—is often a forgotten consideration in a proposed change initiative. An example of this involves comparing the performance of the organization prior to initiating the change versus the performance dreamed about as a result of the proposed change. If, for example, the company is currently losing money, is it realistic to consider that after change the company will be wildly profitable? If the company is currently ineffective, will the change lead the company to be astoundingly effective? While stretch goals may be motivating, moving company performance from zero to infinity is not likely. Employees will be the first to understand this and will as a result either ignore or resist what change management is proposing. In short, employees "ain't buying what management is selling." Successful change managers will understand that there is a wisdom that exists in the crowd and will listen to it for guidance with respect to the practicality of change. Change that lacks *tangibility* also has a way of "losing" the employee population. The way to avoid this is to keep the intangible "dreamy" ideas found in a typical vision and values statement out of the specific strategic initiatives designed to affect change. A company that mixes the vision with the focused execution of change will likely produce a change initiative that lacks the required focus. Some examples of actual company vision statements today include the following:

> "Become one of the leading players in our business areas worldwide and contribute to comfortable home and living environment by expanding new business fields."
> "Connect, Protect, Explore and Inspire the World through.... innovation"
> "To save people money so they can live better."

Each of these statements as compelling and noble as they may be do not provide enough information for driving change. Some questions likely to arise from such statements include:

1. How do we define "leading player"?
2. What is our business area?
3. What do we mean by "new business fields"?

4. What do we mean by "connect"?
5. What category of innovation will be our focus?
6. How will we save money for people?
7. How do we measure the construct "live better"?

Change management efforts must "get real" and focus on credible, practical, clear, and tangible efforts. Fuzzy initiatives that raise too many questions will inevitably lead to the dissipation of the effort expended upon change.

Walk before Running

Unlike many members of the animal kingdom, humans are not able to walk as soon as they are born. In fact, they are not able to sit up, crawl, nor stand. This fact of human development provides a useful perspective for thinking about implementing change. Successful change often begins small, but then leads to successive changes that emerge as a larger, more substantial and complete change. In fact, change managers could do well to view change as a human development effort and seek to progress change through sitting, standing, walking, running, and training. The analog to this could be explained using the example of a process improvement change initiative. To illustrate:

1. Sit: We have identified processes to govern our action.
2. Stand: We have defined the processes to be employed in governing action.
3. Walk: Employees are aware of our processes and know where to find them.
4. Run: Processes are followed even when the context makes it difficult to do so.
5. Train: We seek continuous improvement of processes and work to optimize (Figure 9.12).

In this example, some changes are predecessors for others. It makes no sense to promote process optimization, a late stage emergent state of maturity, when earlier stages of maturity have yet to develop. The word "maturity" is a keyword here and is a long-term prospect for the change

Ad-Hoc Methods	Processes Defined	Processes Implemented	Processes Shared and Communicated	Process Continuous Improvement

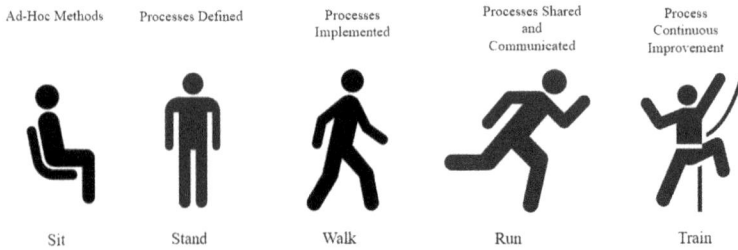

Sit	Stand	Walk	Run	Train

Figure 9.12 Change and process improvement

manager. While the change manager can keep the ideal mature state in mind, the path to the final state must begin with a lower-level initial state. The idea behind "starting small with large-scale initiatives" is frequently observed in industry today. A classic example of this is in the adoption of Agile methodology in project management. Agile is a methodology that seeks to deliver a small element of functionality over time rather than attempting to do it all at once using traditional methods such as the Systems Development Life Cycle or other "waterfall method" approaches. Such methods do not imply that it is wrong to focus on the result. These methods do suggest that the result should be thought of as a destination at the end of a long pathway of stepping stones. While it is true that "those who live in glass houses shouldn't throw stones," change managers should. They should lay out small goals and milestones, or better yet, "inch-pebbles" to set the direction in such a way that the organization walks before running.

Change Action and Governance

There is the saying, "To everything there is a season, and a time to every purpose under the heaven." While the saying is ancient, the idea expressed has implications for change management. Change is best "served warm" when the organization, the market, technology, and the financial situation of the company is right. Further, once the initial diagnosis has been carried out and the organization is prepared, strategic change initiatives should follow naturally. They often do not for various reasons leading to the "hurry up and wait" syndrome led by managers who think that they want to lead change, but are reluctant to take that final step. Perhaps the time doesn't seem right, or the organization doesn't appear to be fully ready. While this may be true, the fact is that there may never be a perfect time for implementing change. Also, failing to act is an act. Not deciding is a decision. Managers who fear the commitment required to undertake change may not be aware of the possibility of carrying out change in phases. Further, the commitment to change may only in practice require a commitment to the initial phase.

Change management taken "one step at a time" could be viewed as a change life cycle, wherein each phase is contemplated, evaluated, executed, and controlled. Each phase is initiated with the approval of a committee of executive sponsors. Such sponsors ensure that proposals meet the entry requirements for each phase and provide budgets, milestones, and deliverable requirements for the phase. The team assigned to the phase proceeds to complete the work of the phase and presents results to the committee of executive sponsors once completed. Also, the team assigned to the change management initiative may call a meeting of sponsors if circumstances warrant it. One example of this is the case in which the team confirms that it is not able to meet committed schedule, budget, or assigned deliverable milestones. When this is the case, the team must report and review status with the committee of sponsors who then proceed to approve, deny, or request additional information. This close interaction with and management by sponsors is known as governance. Companies who employ governance practices are able to act on change quickly while still having the assurance that the change initiatives are tracking to plan and remain in alignment with executive sponsorship.

Project Management and Change Implementation

The term "change initiative" is employed in change management because actions must be carried out and things in one form or another must be delivered in order to bring about change. A change initiative is a temporary activity. It has a clear beginning and end, it is unique, it can be complex, and it employs resources. Therefore, strategic initiatives are projects and may be managed as such. In fact, the beginning activities of a project resemble the activities that must be carried out within the domain of change management. What happens first in a project? The project is officially authorized using a charter and then the "players" who have an interest in the outcome of the project, that is, stakeholders, are identified. What follows is the creation of the project scope. The scope of the project includes both a succinct statement of the scope (what the project will and will not deliver) and a detailed breakdown of all deliverables. The deliverables are then closely examined to identify the activities required to produce the deliverables and the durations are estimated. The activities are sequenced in logical order so that the overall duration of the change initiative is understood. Next, resources are assigned to complete the activities and the costs associated with each resource are attached to the schedule so the budget for the initiative may be generated. These initial steps seem rather like low-level "blocking and tackling" used to develop a schedule. Project management practice goes beyond this low-level sequence of events by including components of a larger plan that are ideal for a holistic implementation of change. Beyond the identification of the scope (i.e., *deliverables*) to be produced, the duration (*schedule*), and resource cost (*budget*), the project management process framework makes available process guidance for every element of a change management initiative. The processes are intended to be incorporated into a series of plans that are integrated together in the "Integration Management Knowledge Area" to form a comprehensive project plan. These processes include the following:

Quality

The quality processes in the project management framework focus the attention of the change management on the requirements of each deliverable. For example, quality management in this context aids the change manager in the quest to identify requirements, create specifications for such requirements, and then verifying that the deliverables meet the specifications. Further, the quality management knowledge area directs the change manager to validate that the deliverables not only meet the specifications of the change initiative, but also meet the original requirements.

Human Resources

The need to motivate and obtain buy-in from team members and organizational stakeholders has already been identified. Project human resource processes do include guidance for team development and motivation—the processes go beyond this by raising additional questions and providing suggestions for answering these questions. For example, change managers consider from where the team members will be acquired. They further think about to what extent team members will be involved in planning and decision-making. Also, once the change is complete, what happens to team members when the change initiative is realized and the team is disbanded? The project management resource processes suggest how managers should arrive at answers to such questions. Also, not all resources in a project are human resources. Equipment, supplies, funding, these are all the resources that a project, in this case, a change initiative manages. How are such resources obtained and management? The project management framework suggests answers.

Communication

Recall that uncertainty, fear, and resistance is the downfall of the change initiative. Change managers intervene in this negative cycle by employing effective communication. The question, however, is "how"? Change managers may send e-mail, hold "all-hands" or departmental "stand-up meetings," employ conference calls, write reports, and the list is endless. Change managers require guidance when it comes to determining the "5 Ws" of communication—Who, What, When, Where, How, and Why. The project management process framework directs particular focus on the "How" and "When." For example, there are categories of communication that are most effective when delivered using one form of media versus another. Depending on the context, an e-mail may be a better fit for delivering a message than a company-wide meeting. Such distinctions in communication media tend to get lost in any project, but are essential factors in a project as important as a change initiative. Finally, effective communication takes quite a bit of work on the part of the change manager. If not careful—as the launch of the completed change initiative approaches—the team leading the initiative may become overwhelmed with collecting data, developing reports, and disseminating them to various stakeholder groups. The creation of a communications plan early in the project can streamline the overall communication effort so that the right message goes to the right place and time without tying up more resources than necessary.

Risk

There is the old saying that "if anything can go wrong—it will go wrong." The fact that a change initiative exists suggests that something somewhere went wrong and something new must be developed in order to address the problem or provide course correct. Further, the change initiative that gets planned may be derailed by unanticipated circumstances. The project management framework offers a step-by-step approach to incorporating thinking about risks and dealing with risks within a change initiative. In a project, risks are identified, assessed, and ranked. Once ranked, response plans for risks are considered and adopted. Why develop response plans after risks are ranked? This is because managers leading projects and initiatives cannot track all possible risks. Instead, managers focus on those risks deemed to be most important. Responses to risks include mitigation, avoid, retain, and transfer. Mitigation is a response that seeks to minimize the impact of a risk should it materialize. Risks are avoided when teams take alternative paths that do not exhibit the risk that is identified. A risk considered to be manageable and more expensive to mitigate than simply accepted is said to be retained risk. Finally, project management processes include guidance for assigning risks to third parties. This is referred to as risk transfer and may involve compensation in return for assigning risks. Typically, this takes the form of insurance or contractual terms.

Procurement

Change initiatives can and often do require resources from outside the company. This may involve labor, equipment, technology, or something as significant as an enterprise resource planning system. Managers focused on change may lack experience with matters such as vendor identification, vendor selection, and contract management. Furthermore, the day-to-day informal interaction of carrying out work and exchanging deliverables between functional groups within the company may not sufficiently support the day-to-day management of an outside vendor. The project management process framework aids in filling in the gaps in skills and experience of the manager so that procurement elements within the change initiative may operate smoothly.

Stakeholder

The players involved in the change initiative are known as stakeholders. Stakeholders may be those on the team or those who will be affected in some way by the change. The idea of the stakeholder goes beyond participation and impact. Stakeholders include those who may have an interest in the outcome of the initiative. Interested parties may or may not support the initiative, and this is one reason why the team leading the initiative understand who these individuals are so that they can be engaged. Engagement may act to reduce the negative impact of those who do not favor the project, but engagement may also lead to the shifting of stakeholders from the "opposition" to the "supporter" camp. The question for the change manager is "how"? The project management process framework provides a number of suggested tools and techniques for identifying, analyzing, ranking in order of importance, and engaging stakeholders. Since change management primarily involves marshaling the time, energy, skills, and emotions of organizational stakeholders, it could be said that project management process guidance for stakeholders is one of the most important areas of guidance for the manager of change initiatives (Figure 9.13).

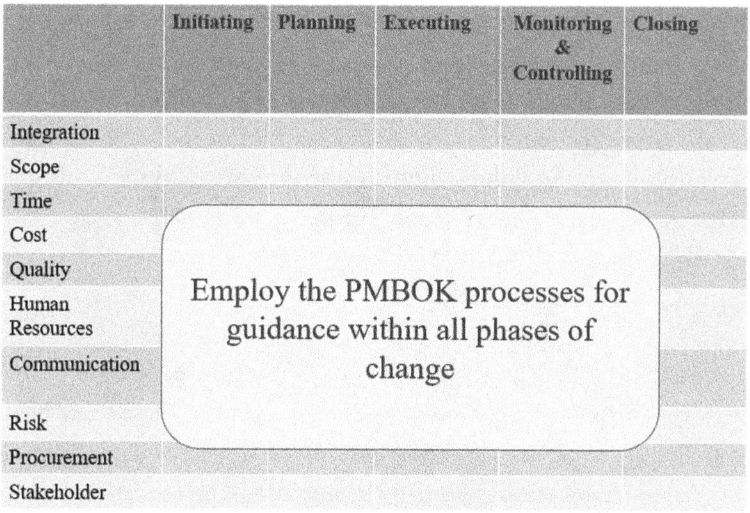

	Initiating	Planning	Executing	Monitoring & Controlling	Closing
Integration					
Scope					
Time					
Cost					
Quality					
Human Resources		Employ the PMBOK processes for guidance within all phases of change			
Communication					
Risk					
Procurement					
Stakeholder					

Figure 9.13 Change and project management

Project Management Process Summary

It is observed that change initiatives are often highly involved, complex activities that cut across functional domains within a company, internal and external stakeholders, vendors, and even customers. The possibility of going offtrack, missing the mark in terms of requirements, going over budget, or getting behind schedule is sufficiently high that the initiative must be closely managed. Some change managers will be more experienced at managing complexity than others. Since change initiatives fit the definition of a project given its temporary nature and focus on tangible deliverables, the project management process framework provides a compass that points the way toward how to build, manage, and control a complete plan.

The Change Life Cycle

The "change initiative as project" view leads to the understanding that a change initiative follows an overall life cycle. An example of a change life cycle is described as follows:

Phase 1: Feasibility

In this phase, change triggers are evaluated and reviewed with the committee of executive sponsors, and if considered sufficient to warrant further action, a study was initiated to evaluate the trigger event in more detail, outline the nature of the change required to meet the challenge, and finally assess the ability of the organization as well as the availability of resources to carry out the action (Figure 9.14).

Phase 2: Plan

If the output of the change feasibility phase is approved, the committee of executive sponsors then charters the change plan phase. This phase identifies the required deliverables, activities required to implement the deliverables, milestones, resource assignments, and budget. At the end of the plan phase, the committee once again reviews the output, considers the overall business need, and yet again ensures that the change continues

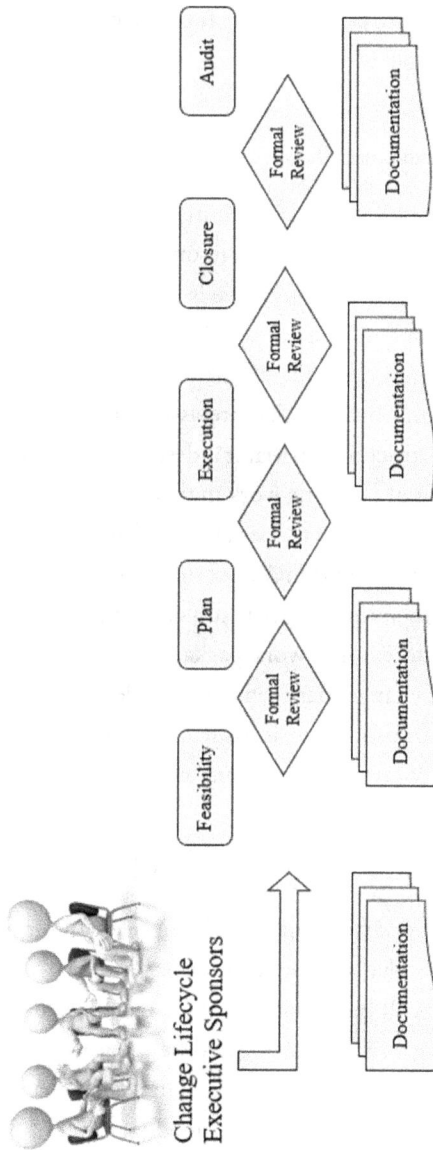

Figure 9.14 *The change management life cycle*

to make sense in terms of strategic alignment. The end of the plan phase is likely to be the most daunting for executives. This is because up to this point, change implementation was under consideration and minimal resources and budget have been assigned. If the plan is approved, this means that execution will follow.

Phase 3: The Execution Phase

When change is executed, the change initiatives that are identified receive the go-ahead to be assigned to those resources who carry out the work. Often the work of the change initiative is assigned, monitored, and controlled using the work assignment tool known as the work package. The work package contains a bundle of related deliverables, activities, durations, milestones, and budgets that are assigned to individuals or small teams. The work is structured so that it is designed to be completed within 2 weeks. The benefit of assigning work in this way is that the change manager can closely manage all activities and confirm progress. Work that is designed to be completed within 2 weeks lends itself to frequent checking and updating. Further, the budget is sufficiently granular so that spending is closely monitored. The work package example illustrates how the execution phase of change management is carried out. Execution in this case is bundling work so that it is easily assigned and tracked, and then following up with controls as well as any necessary course correct.

Phase 4: Closure, Handover, and Lessons Learned

Once the work of the change initiative is completed, it is formally ended by reviewing the results with the committee of executive sponsors. Part of the final review will be capturing the lessons learned from the initiative and identifying which lessons could be incorporated into new processes, procedures, or policies associated with change management. Once this is accomplished, the development of the proposed change is complete. Consistent with Lewin's concept of "refreezing," the result of the initiative—be it a new process, new reporting structure, or implementation of new technology—is formally handed over to functional groups. It is the functional groups within the organization that use the result of the change initiative with the goal in mind of incorporating it (i.e., "refreez-ing") into day-to-day life.

Phase 5: Audit

Change initiatives are ushered in with a flurry of activity and excitement. Once the proposed change is complete and is implemented, the excite-ment dies down. The possibility exists that the organization may forget what has been learned and soon fall back into the old way of doing things. One way to ensure that this does not happen is to schedule a change audit 3, 6, 9, and 12 months after handover to ensure that "refreezing" has oc-curred, and that the organization has indeed changed. In the course of carrying out the audit, it may be discovered that the change as originally envisioned is less than ideal. This may lead to new change proposals, in which case a new phase 1 feasibility proposal is put forward for review.

The Change Management Roadmap

The fact that change follows a life cycle and is governed at the most senior level of the organization suggests that executives could consider change as a long-term exercise that is managed in a manner similar to the concept of continuous improvement in quality management. Also, the idea of a roadmap is a term that is also used in research and development and product management organizations. In the context of R&D and prod-uct development, the roadmap identifies what products the organization intends to deliver over the midterm—typically 3 to 5 years. Products are proposed on the roadmap based on the current understanding of the ex-pected trajectory of the industry, market, and macroenvironment. While products are the "end-game" of the roadmap exercise, products are re-alized by a highly developed supporting infrastructure of technologies, components, platforms, people, and support systems.

It is possible for executives to consider long-term change goals in a manner similar to a product roadmap. Like the product roadmap, execu-tives consider the trajectory of the market and macroeconomic trends and use this understanding to determine what is required of the organi-zation to be successful in the future business environment. While future products rely on significant underlying components, technologies, platforms, and systems, future change also relies on significant underlying support systems and infrastructure. To use an analogy, whereas the change anticipated to be required in the future could be viewed as the "tip of the iceberg," executives spend the years leading up to the change by building the elements of the iceberg that are found under the waterline. These elements include people, skills, know-how, systems, organizational structure, and technologies. Each of these elements could be envisioned, chartered, executed, and integrated over time. The change roadmap could be employed as a component of the annual strategic planning process. It is natural to conclude that some course corrections would be applied within each annual strategic planning cycle. Also, the plan would naturally respond to discontinuities in the market and macroenvironment. However, the chances of failure to change as well as failed change would likely be lower when a company employs the change roadmap approach. This is because change would never be a surprise. Instead, the roadmap would function more like a long-term building project. One common means for envisioning roadmap style long-term change is through the use of the process maturity model. Change is inherent in growth and maturity, and process improvement is an important long-term change goal. One such maturity model is one pioneered by PRTM. This model includes components of the PACE (Product and Cycle Time Excellence) methodology (Figure 9.15).

Change Management and the PMO

Since change initiatives are projects, they follow a life cycle, and they can be linked together into a long-term roadmap, and it follows that change initiatives could benefit from a PMO (project management office) within the organization. A PMO takes different forms and may play different roles depending on the strategy and scale of the organization. The smallest instance of a PMO is an organization with one or more project managers who provide expert process guidance and templates for change initiatives and other projects implemented throughout the organization. A more mature instance of a PMO envisions the organization as a functional group where all of the project managers of the organization

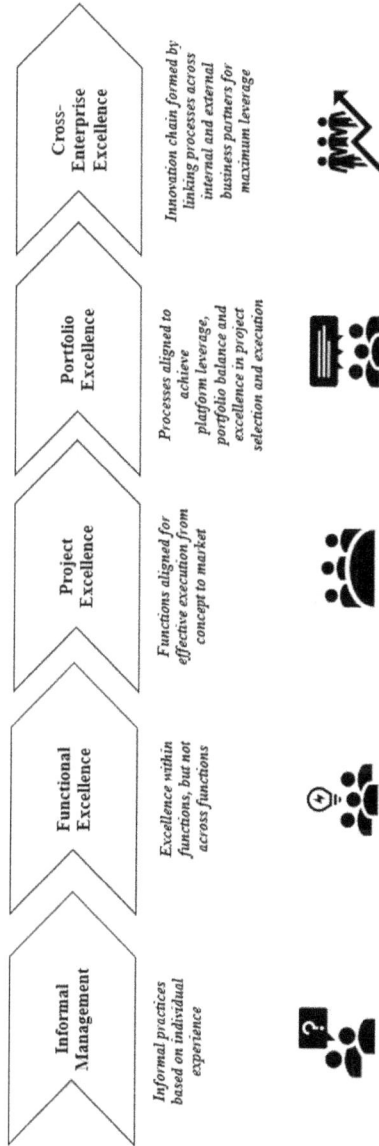

Informal Management

Informal practices based on individual experience

Functional Excellence

Excellence within functions, but not across functions

Project Excellence

Functions aligned for effective execution from concept to market

Portfolio Excellence

Processes aligned to achieve platform leverage, portfolio balance and excellence in project selection and execution

Cross-Enterprise Excellence

Innovation chain formed by linking processes across internal and external business partners for maximum leverage

Figure 9.15 The long-term change roadmap

Source: McGrath and Romeri (1994).

reside. Projects reaching an established financial threshold are assigned a project manager from the PMO. In addition, the PMO in this case is a repository of project management software tools, templates, and lessons learned guidance collected over the years and made available for retrieval. Finally, an advanced PMO may also lead the project and change initiative governance function. The committee of executive sponsors that functions as the decision-making body in change life cycle phases is either led or organized by the PMO director. Regardless of specific assignment in this governance scheme, it is the PMO that owns the life cycle and governance process for change initiatives and projects (Figure 9.16).

Do We Really Want to Fail?

It is safe to assume that no one wants to fail, yet companies do this every day when they attempt change. What then should managers do in order to succeed? Don't do what is likely to guarantee failure. To review, consider **DON'T** versus **DO**. The failed experiences of others provide a change management checklist that can help managers stop dead in their tracks prior to embarking upon the wrong move. Looking back, the following pointers are observed:

Failing to understand what needs to be changed
   DON'T: Perform a surface analysis of problems faced by the company.
   DO: Carefully perform an in-depth diagnosis of company problems.
   DON'T: Adopt a narrow viewpoint while thinking "inside the box."
   DO: Seek to employ a wide perspective so that creative options become recognized.
   DON'T: Assume that the application of your traditional strengths and know-how will solve the problem.
   DO: Consider that you may be facing unique problems that extend beyond the previous know-how that resides within the company.
   DON'T: Assume that leadership skill is a cure-all for organizational problems.
   DO: Consider that the change context may require domain expertise and technical know-how as a required component of leadership.
   DON'T: Make a strategic personnel decision without seeking counsel first.

Oversight of Change Initiatives

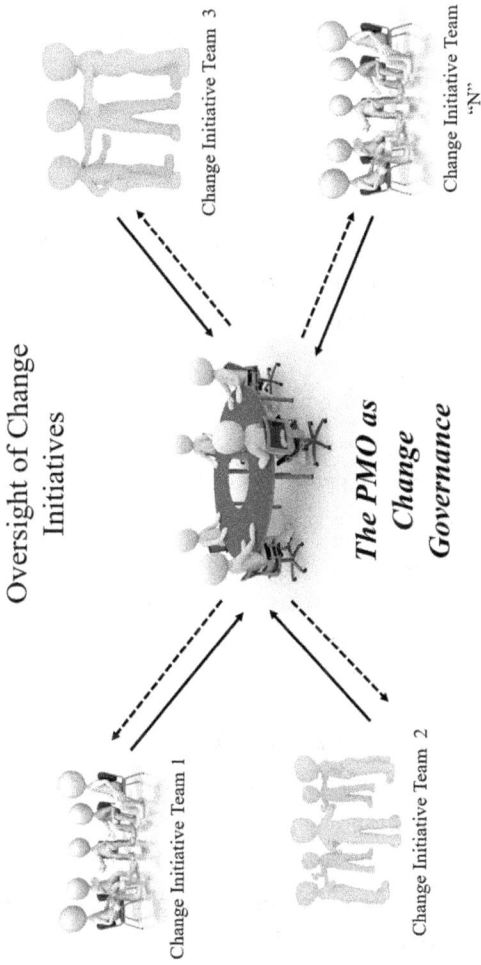

Change Initiative Team 3

Change Initiative Team "N"

The PMO as Change Governance

Change Initiative Team 1

Change Initiative Team 2

Figure 9.16 *Oversight of change initiatives*

DO: Counsel stakeholders who are affected by a change in leadership.

DON'T: Propose only change initiatives that are aligned with your functional background.

DO: Draw upon the expertise of others outside your domain of expertise as a means of considering solution alternatives.

Solving the wrong problem

DON'T: Make causal connections that aren't there.

DO: Seek to understand the true underlying causal linkages between actions and results.

DON'T: Uncritically accept the judgment of consultants.

DO: Use consultant recommendations as one of many inputs when evaluating the nature of the problem and possible solutions.

DON'T: Assume that an expert in one field can contribute expert work in a completely different field (especially when the expert is an engineer).

DO: Recognize that different functional domains have specific skill sets and knowledge base that go beyond what may be offered by a manager with demonstrated general intelligence.

DON'T: Address process and execution problems by cheering on management staff.

DO: Avoid glossing over problems and issues with positive gloss and instead focus on communicating the nuts and bolts of problems and solutions.

Solving a perceived rather than a real problem

DON'T: Apply a management theory or practice because it is promoted by a notable academic.

DO: Use academic theory as one of many sources of evidence and guidance used for understanding the phenomena associated with the problem to be addressed.

DON'T: Create the appearance of a successful global company rather than be one.

DO: Seek to understand the underlying policies, processes, and procedures that facilitate the successful operation of a global company.

DON'T: Take steps to achieve the illusion of control rather than actual control.

DO: Openly explain and document the real decision-making authority boundaries available to managers in the organization.

DON'T: Take steps to address an issue that bothers you, and in doing so reduce the effectiveness of the company.

DO: Adopt a holistic view and seek to change issues that affect the overall performance of the company.

The wrong solution for the right problem

DON'T: Solve small problems when you are not able to solve large ones.

DO: Face the reality of the large-scale barriers to success that exist in the firm and address them head-on.

DON'T: Actively snuff out the expertise of a company that was acquired … for its expertise.

DO: Employ the expertise obtained in an acquisition to advance the strategy of the company.

DON'T: Always do exactly what clients tell you to do.

DO: Think about what clients are saying and seek to understand the underlying issues that are steering the activity of the client.

Transplanting a change solution from another company

DON'T: Introduce a compensation scheme from a company operating in a different context, culture, industry, or all of the above.

DO: Carefully study the context and culture of the company so that proposed compensation schemes align with strategy and change initiatives.

DON'T: Eliminate management layers so as to emulate a previous company operating in a different context, culture, industry, or all of the above.

DO: Think first about what the existing company needs prior to implementing practices or organizational designs originating in other companies.

DON'T: Insist that senior managers keep busy with operational tasks rather than strategic decision-making.

DO: Ensure that each level in the organization is performing the work that is appropriate for its authority and responsibility.

DON'T: Transplant a process or methodology from a familiar to an alien context.

DO: Evaluate the context of the solution to be applied prior to adopting it.

SMART versus DUMB goals

DON'T: Advocate for questionable, out of context change initiatives.

DO: Seek counsel on change ideas prior to their implementation.

DON'T: Promote the adoption of practices loosely defined by buzzwords.

DO: Insist on clear, direct, and focused communications accompanied by definitions for all terms employed in the workplace.

DON'T: Pursue markets because they are large.

DO: Pursue markets that have the potential to be profitable in light of Porter's guidelines.

DON'T: Implement a new organizational design without explaining how it is supposed to work.

DO: Understand the "nuts and bolts" of the operation to the point that it can be clearly articulated to the organization.

DON'T: Enter a new market with a new product.

DO: Avoid striking out into the unknown as an act of desperation. Think first, then do.

DON'T: Analyze a change decision until the opportunity has passed.

DO: Understand that no decision is a decision already made.

Double down on what used to work

DON'T: Do what you know how to do rather than what the market requires you to do.

DO: Understand that was successful in the past may not be successful in the present.

DON'T: Do exactly what you previously did that worked in another time and context, but this time only harder.

DO: A strategy that is no longer appropriate in the present is likely to continue to be inappropriate, even if the strategy is pursued with additional vigor.

DON'T: Narrowly define what it is that your company does to limit opportunities to evolve.

DO: Widen the lens in which the company and its playing field is viewed so that opportunities to evolve are not missed.

DON'T: Fail to grasp the current means for attaining a competitive advantage in the marketplace.

DO: See the marketplace in terms of competitive advantage opportunity in terms of Porter's framework.

GOBASH

DON'T: Overestimate future sales growth.

DO: Seek counsel in forecasts and liberally apply realism.

DON'T: Assume that a market that is growing today will continue to grow tomorrow.

DO: Understand that all markets have life cycles.

DON'T: Go big with major fixed cost investments because others are doing it.

DO: Understand that the stampede of competition may be headed for a cliff. Avoid the temptation to join them.

DON'T: Assume that an ERP system implementation will save the company.

DO: Understand that an ERP system is a highly complex and expensive undertaking that may or may not help the company advance strategic interests.

Betting the company on the big idea

DON'T: Readily introduce popular foreign products who use case is not fully understood.

DO: Carefully consider how customers might use an unfamiliar product in their day-to-day lives.

DON'T: Believe the following "Runaway successes in other countries will lead to success, change, and transformation if introduced in a different country."

DO: Recognize that a success in one culture may not readily transfer to a different culture.

DON'T: Trust rosy forecasts for the new product and prepare accordingly.

DO: Follow evidence born of the study of market trends, customer feedback, and the product life cycle.

DON'T: Uncritically accept focus group data on proposed new products.

DO: Vet focus group evidence by comparing with other sources of data.

DON'T: Implement that pet "big idea" as soon as the opportunity presents itself.

DO: Recognize that the best idea for the company may not involve the promotion of your "big idea."

The savior from the outside

DON'T: Assume that the expertise of the outsider is a good fit.

DO: Critically evaluate the experience and track record of the outsider.

DON'T: Believe that the outsider understands the company.

DO: Seek corroborating evidence that the outsider has a grasp of the market, the competition, and the unique issues faced by the company.

DON'T: Accept what the outsider tells you at face value during the recruiting process.

DO: Ask probing questions in all interactions and interviews during the hiring process to uncover gaps in candidate understanding and background.

DON'T: Be attracted to the unfamiliar.

DO: Recognize that what is new will become less attractive the better that it is understood. Understand that this is likely to happen quickly in an unfamiliar and risky market.

Successful growth and change by M&A

DON'T: Acquire a major competitor during the final stages of market decline.

DO: Retool prior to market collapse and leave what remains to competitors.

DON'T: Assume that customer buying patterns will not change in the absence of multiple competitors in the marketplace.

DO: Appreciate that the market is dynamic rather than static and that customers will respond to market shifts as they inevitably act in their own interest.

DON'T: Overlook the expense of maintaining and supporting acquired product lines.

DO: Be conservative when estimating how much money an acquisition is likely to save the company in practice.

DON'T: Build a larger company with a collection of smaller companies that seek to lead rather than follow the lead of the acquirer.

DO: Assess the cultural fit of target acquisitions and clearly identify and plan roles and responsibilities after acquisition.

Failure to implement

DON'T: Commit to change without understanding the implications to executive management.

DO: Present a realistic roadmap that clarifies the role of senior and executive management, including the constraints associated with required process discipline.

DON'T: Promote change that requires managers to do what they are never going to do.

DO: Expect that managers will act in their own best interest, and seek to understand what that is.

DON'T: Embark on change that ignores the culture, history, and fundamental capability of the company.

DO: Take incremental steps that the company can achieve.

DON'T: Attempt change on a grand scale with managers having only small-scale experience.

DO: Understand the background and experience level of managers who will be leading the change effort.

While the "Do" directives seem obvious compared to the "Don'ts," in the heat of the moment when responding to a change trigger with a plan, the fact is that the "Dos" are never as obvious as they may appear at face value. Change initiatives fail more often than they succeed, making it clear that the quick and thoughtless path is the most likely path, and the "Do" directives have proven over time to be the "road not taken." For managers, this infers that every change endeavor presents the manager with a fork in the road. When the fork is apparent, stop, look, and think, then choose "Do" over "Don't" every time. Success is not guaranteed, but perhaps more likely.

Assessing Change Capability

An examination of the list of "Don'ts" reveals patterns to the mistakes that change managers often make. To illustrate this point, each of the list of "Don'ts" was uploaded to a word-cloud generator that analyzes text and weights words by their frequency. The word cloud is observed to emphasize a number of keywords for which change managers should pay close attention (Figure 9.17).

Figure 9.17 The keyword word cloud

The keywords of interest are:

Assume	Context	Expert	Outsider
Culture	Expertise	Different	Process
Uncritically	Lead	Decision-making	Market

These notable keywords occur more frequently than others found in the extensive list of "Don't" words. While they are related to the many other words found in the word cloud, they do provide interesting waypoints for managers to think about and avoid when embarking upon change. As a result, they may be used to assess the success potential for a change initiative. A straightforward method for carrying out such an assessment is to create a simple survey instrument. The survey instrument measures the level of agreement with statements linked to the keywords resulting from the analysis of the "Don't" list. A suggested "Change Success Assessment Instrument" is given below:

1. My change initiative is grounded in my own assumptions regarding what is needed.
   a. Strongly agree
   b. Agree
   c. Neither agree nor disagree
   d. Disagree
   e. Strongly disagree
2. I have given the context of the proposed change limited in-depth consideration.
   a. Strongly agree
   b. Agree
   c. Neither agree nor disagree
   d. Disagree
   e. Strongly disagree
3. I have faith in experts who provide the change recommendations.
   a. Strongly agree
   b. Agree
   c. Neither agree nor disagree
   d. Disagree
   e. Strongly disagree
4. I have brought in outsiders to lead the proposed change.
   a. Strongly agree
   b. Agree
   c. Neither agree nor disagree
   d. Disagree
   e. Strongly disagree
5. I have given limited consideration of the company culture.
   a. Strongly agree
   b. Agree

   c. Neither agree nor disagree

   d. Disagree

   e. Strongly disagree

6. I am confident in my expertise to know what change the company needs.

   a. Strongly agree

   b. Agree

   c. Neither agree nor disagree

   d. Disagree

   e. Strongly disagree

7. The new path I have proposed for the company is significantly different from the previous direction.

   a. Strongly agree

   b. Agree

   c. Neither agree nor disagree

   d. Disagree

   e. Strongly disagree

8. I have limited experience in process improvement

   a. Strongly agree

   b. Agree

   c. Neither agree nor disagree

   d. Disagree

   e. Strongly disagree

9. I have uncritically accepted a proposal for a new direction for the company.

   a. Strongly agree

   b. Agree

   c. Neither agree nor disagree

   d. Disagree

   e. Strongly disagree

10. The leadership of my company has limited change experience.

   a. Strongly agree

   b. Agree

   c. Neither agree nor disagree

   d. Disagree

   e. Strongly disagree

11. Decision-making is a serious weakness within my company.
    a. Strongly agree
    b. Agree
    c. Neither agree nor disagree
    d. Disagree
    e. Strongly disagree
12. I have limited experience within the market associated with the proposed change initiative.
    a. Strongly agree
    b. Agree
    c. Neither agree nor disagree
    d. Disagree
    e. Strongly disagree
13. I discovered the idea for the change from a popular management book.
    a. Strongly agree
    b. Agree
    c. Neither agree nor disagree
    d. Disagree
    e. Strongly disagree
14. My change initiative relies on the acquisition of a competitor
    a. Strongly agree
    b. Agree
    c. Neither agree nor disagree
    d. Disagree
    e. Strongly disagree
15. My change initiative relies on the implementation of an ERP system.
    a. Strongly agree
    b. Agree
    c. Neither agree nor disagree
    d. Disagree
    e. Strongly disagree

The simple survey may be scored by using "strongly agree = 5" and "strongly disagree = 1." When the survey is administered, scored, and tabulated, a score greater than the mean score of 3 suggests that from the failed change experiences of others the planned change initiative may require additional scrutiny and "shoring up" of weaknesses. Where should a change manager begin to shore up such weaknesses? Focus on the twelve keywords and the list of change management "Don'ts" that form the basis of each survey question. The keywords are linked to the "pointers for how to fail "don't" list," which, if avoided, increase the opportunity for successful change.

Change and Career Implications

It is no secret that executive and CEO pay is very high, particularly for those who have a track record of success. A key reason for this is that large-scale value creation activities are many and the pool of those who can lead them and produce the results desired by shareholders are few. The price for such talent is therefore bid up into the tens of millions of dollars per year depending on the size and scale of the company. The general public sees the money made by such executives, but may not see as clearly the level of difficulty of the management effort as well as the constant need for the management of problem-solving and change leadership required by the executive. A successful executive is not something that one is, but it is rather something that one "does." A key element of this is change management. While it can be fun to be in charge and give orders to subordinates, successfully guiding a company over a period of years consists more of hard work than fun. The company 10 years from now may need to be quite a different company than it is today. It is observed that arriving at this new state is very difficult and goes far beyond giving orders. Some naturally gifted CEOs and change agents may have a vision of where to take the company and instinctively understand how to get there. Most, on the other hand, will understand the importance of process in change management. They will appreciate the need for the company to evolve, but at the same time, will pay careful attention to detail and take into account those factors that tend to get missed when acting in the heat of the moment. While successful CEOs have a reputation for acting quickly, the ones who rise to the top have depth. They take the time to bypass the "Don'ts" and instead adopt the "Dos." The success CEO thrives on the rapid change of the business world of the information age. When the market shifts, they have done their homework and the companies they lead are ready to meet the challenge. They do not fail at change management (Figure 9.18).

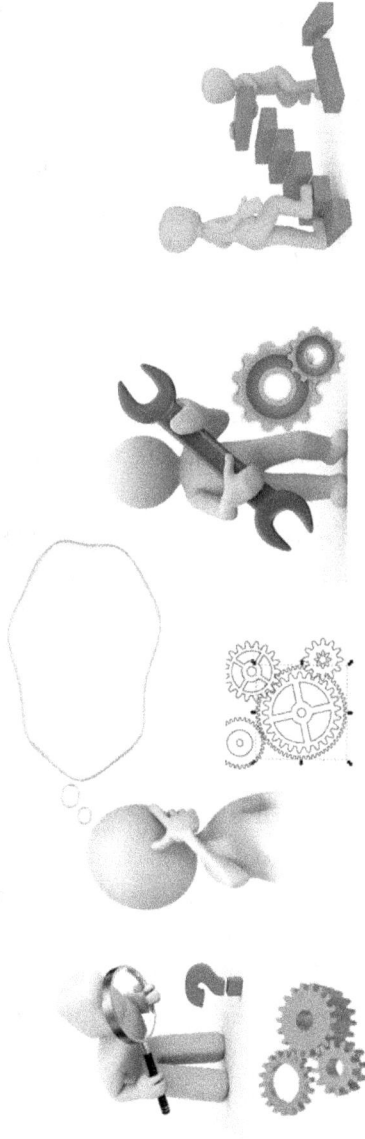

Identifying the right problems   **Getting the analysis right**   **Implementing the right change initiatives**   **Taking it to the next level**

Figure 9.18 Career progress

131

Final Advice for the Change Manager

For many years, the highlight of the week in popular radio was Kasey Kasem's American Top 40. Reruns of this weekly countdown continue today on YouTube and Internet radio. Kasey ended each episode with a saying that change managers would do well to incorporate. The saying goes, "Keep your feet on the ground, but keep reaching for the stars." The interesting aspect of this phrase is that it is often easy to either keep one's feet on the ground or to reach for the stars. Rarely, however, is it easy to do both at once? Keeping "feet on the ground" evokes the idea of a static existence that focuses on living according to the strategy, policies, procedures, and processes of today. Businesses with the right strategy thrive by keeping "feet on the ground." Jim Collins of "Built to Last" and "Good to Great" fame reinforces the idea of the "flywheel" effect in running a business. Using this analogy, Collins outlines the importance of "sticking to one's knitting" and staying the course over the long term. The message is that doing what one is best at will eventually pay off and companies observed to be successful over the long run practice this. The problem with "keep feet on the ground" is that in today's market, eventually the ground will shift, thereby toppling whoever has remained standing. Long-term survival requires change and a rejection of the comfort that comes with a static existence.

Reaching for the stars, on the other hand, evokes change and novelty. It is the novelty of change that is attractive and often a temptation for CEOs who jump at the chance to adopt a novel position without adequate thought regarding the hidden dangers, the implications to the company, and the costs involved in change. A CEO who gravitates toward change and dynamic and rapid evolution would do well to examine the lessons of change management history, adopt the "Dos," and avoid the "Don'ts."

Change, in the venerable words of Kasey Kasem, is about the balance between the static and the dynamic. A company must "reach," but at the same time reach wisely so that the success and know-how of past accomplishment is preserved. You now know how to fail at change management, now go forward and seek to succeed.

Bibliography

Jurevicius, O. 2013. "McKinsey 7S Model." *Strategic Management Insight.* https://strategicmanagementinsight.com/tools/mckinsey-7s-model -framework.html (accessed December 12, 2019).

Lewin, K. 1947. "Frontiers in Group Dynamics: II. Channels of Group Life; Social Planning and Action Research." *Human Relations* 1, no. 2, pp. 143–153. doi: 10.1177/001872674700100201

McGrath, M. E., and M. N. Romeri. 1994. "The R&D Effectiveness Index: A Metric for Product Development Performance." *Journal of Product Innovation Management* 11, no. 3, pp. 213–220.

Prosci (2019). ADKAR Change Management Model Overview: Prosci. Retrieved from https://www.prosci.com/adkar/adkar-model (accessed 19th December 2019).

Senge, P. M. 1997. "The Fifth Discipline." *Measuring Business Excellence* 1, no. 3, pp. 46–51.

About the Authors

Dr James W. Marion is a tenured associate professor at Embry–Riddle Aeronautical University Worldwide. He is currently the department chair of the College of Business, Department of Decision Sciences. His experience includes leading large organizations in multiple product launches in the United States, Europe, and Asia. Dr Marion has a PhD in organization and management with a specialization in information technology management from Capella University. He holds an MS in engineering from the University of Wisconsin–Platteville and an MSc and MBA in strategic planning as well as a postgraduate certificate in business research methods from the Edinburgh Business School at Heriot-Watt University. He is a certified project management professional (PMP).

John Lewis is a developer, system architect, and computer enthusiast who has been keenly interested in electronics at an early age. He earned an advanced Ham radio license at the age of 15 and in 1979 received the FCC First Class Radio Telephone Operator License, which then was required for the repair and adjustment of FCC licensed radio transmitters including broadcast TV. He was instrumental in the startup of two successful businesses in the electronics and mechanical fields. John is currently a lead member of architecture at AT&T, where over the past 30 years he has received more than 100 US patents on his ideas in the communications field. He attended the State Technical Institute in Memphis, Grantham College of Engineering, and the then Memphis State University to further his knowledge in the field of communication.

Index

OTHER TITLES IN OUR PORTFOLIO AND PROJECT MANAGEMENT COLLECTION

Timothy Kloppenborg, *Editor*

- *Project Management Essentials, Second Edition* by Kathryn N. Wells and Timothy J. Kloppenborg
- *Passion, Persistence, and Patience: Key Skills for Achieving Project Success* by Alfonso Bucero
- *Implementing Information Systems Projects: A Managerial Perspective* by D P Goyal
- *Adaptive Project Planning* by Christopher Worsley
- *Project Portfolio Management, Second Edition: A Model for Improved Decision Making* by Clive N. Enoch
- *The Lost Art of Planning Projects* by Louise Worsley and Christopher Worsley
- *Project Communication from Start to Finish: The Dynamics of Organizational Success* by Geraldine E. Hynes
- *Executing Global Projects: A Practical Guide to Applying the PMBOK Framework in the Global Environment* by James Marion and Tracey Richardson
- *Capital Project Management, Volume I: Capital Project Strategy* by Robert N. McGrath
- *Capital Project Management, Volume II: Capital Project Finance* by Robert N. McGrath
- *Capital Project Management, Volume III: Evolutionary Forces* by Robert N. McGrath
- *Projects, Programs, and Portfolios in Strategic Organizational Transformation* by James Jiang and Gary Klein

Announcing the Business Expert Press Digital Library

Concise e-books business students need for classroom and research

This book can also be purchased in an e-book collection by your library as

- *a one-time purchase,*
- *that is owned forever,*
- *allows for simultaneous readers,*
- *has no restrictions on printing, and*
- *can be downloaded as PDFs from within the library community.*

Our digital library collections are a great solution to beat the rising cost of textbooks. E-books can be loaded into their course management systems or onto students' e-book readers. The **Business Expert Press** digital libraries are very affordable, with no obligation to buy in future years. For more information, please visit **www.businessexpertpress.com/librarians**. To set up a trial in the United States, please email **sales@businessexpertpress.com**.

www.ingramcontent.com/pod-product-compliance
Lightning Source LLC
Chambersburg PA
CBHW061324220326
41599CB00026B/5027